Hashferay Prison:
Memories of a Prisoner

Sammy Sium (K.Mariam)

ISBN: 1517760992
ISBN-13: 978-1517760991

DEDICATION

This work is dedicated to those who are been jailed in Eritrea without crime and charges; to those who died due to torture.

PREFACE

This book is a collection of things I witnessed when I was a prisoner of conscience in Hashferay prison, Eritrea. It is by no means a complete work and I am sure many inhumane crimes were committed before and after my time. But it is my duty to share what I lived first-hand and what I heard what happened before I have arrived. Even though I kept dates of the major events that took place, there is a chance some might be wrong because finding a pen and a piece of paper was not easy.

I do hope this little contribution gives the readers a picture of the inhumane acts done over Eritrean's of all ages and gender in the name of rehabilitation. It is my strong hope that former prisoners of Hashferay contribute to this work and make it a complete work for the next generation and most importantly, educate readers about the cruel and miserable military detention centers of Eritrea run by the current dictatorial regime.

For any information, please email me at kmsium@gmail.com

Happy reading!

Sammy Sium

THE BEGINNING

My journey to Hashferay prison started from my dream of been a free citizen who can study, work and basically exist like a normal human being should. In January 2013, I found a study opportunity in Europe. But like every other youth in the country, I wasn't allowed to make use of the opportunity I found after a lot of submissions and searches. At that time, I was rotten in the national slavery program named national service for nearly 7 years. Don't get me wrong; I had more freedom than the soldiers whose life has stopped moving forward years ago, than the educated youth forced to look after some military commander's animals. No, I was doing my national service right in the heart of the capital. I was eating my mother's food and sleeping in my cozy bed.

But still I was a slave. I was earning fifty cents per month for the first 13 months of my national service. Then an increase came up and I was making less than $5 dollars per month for God knows how long. But that's not the catch of it all. I was somebody else's property. I wasn't supposed to plan and ultimately dream. The future was already written for me and I had to accept it. And I did so for seven years. I still don't know how I let precious years get wasted for nothing.

And the very first and biggest mistake I did was for not fighting for my freedom in the early years of my slavery. I stopped dreaming of the future because I was lost in the little more than usual freedom I had. I believed when my boss said "Once we get a replacement, we will release from your national service and you can follow your choices". I should have known better. I had seen many dreams and plans been crushed, many morals evaporating into nothing and mostly, many lies been told and re-told since the day I became an official object of the government.

I should have taken an action to free myself sooner when I saw my former classmates, friends and collogues who escaped the regime making real progress in their life, reaching out to their potential and dreams with no authority telling them to remain stagnant. No, I simply went on being a slave whose dreams of freedom and better life was getting further and further.

But then, now, I have something to talk about. Though under pressure and with passion that was lost long ago, I did serve my country and my people. Not everything went to waste except my youth and the precious time I was jailed for wanting to serve myself.

When I was told "no" to my request to be released from the national service, I decided to flee the country. My first plan was to escape to Khartoum, Sudan. It was then I approached my good friend Bereket, who escaped to Khartoum around February 2013. He was excited about the plan and promised to arrange a trusted and qualified smuggler to smuggle me out of Eritrea to Sudan. Within three days, Bereket got back to me with goods news that he had found a very experienced and trusted smuggler for 160,000.00Nfa (around $3000.00 at that time) from a town called Barentu to Khartoum, Sudan. I trust Bereket so much so I agreed to his demands without any question. The day of departure was unknown so we set a code that would mean "go to Barentu". The code was he would call and say "Say hi to your family"

I didn't wait for the call for long. After three days, on Tuesday, he called me at eight in the evening and said the code. I did have some unfinished things but none was as important as leaving that day. Busses to Barentu leave around 5am and so I decided to put closure to some important things and sleep. But sleep was far from sight. It was understandable, at least from my perspective. It was hard to be at ease knowing I was traveling 200km to meet a smuggler who I have no idea about. Smugglers are mostly stone and cold hearted people who make selfish decisions. They also lie about their experience and safety measures all because they are mainly obsessed with the money they are going to make. Around 3am, I did sleep but woke up shortly at 4:30 by my mobile.

That morning was particularly tough. I had to go to the kitchen. My mother was sleeping in the next room and she could hear me moving stuff. We were very close and she did know I wanted to leave but saying good bye was out of the question and tough. I knew her days would be full of worries and so I just left without saying a thing.

I was used to walking the streets of Asmara between midnight and 6am since I often arrive home from work around 5am. But that morning, it felt different. For once I realized I am leaving Asmara, the city I was born and lived for nearly thirty years yet barely knew. My memories of the city were very, very limited and many of its places were unheard of and unseen to me. Worse yet, no one except one immediate family was aware of my leaving plans. And so, as I walk from Bagaliano to the bus stop, I began wondering of all the friendships I could have built and the things I could have done and seen. But now it was over and so, I just prayed that my escape is successful and the next cities are going to be as kind as Asmara to me.

The bus stop was very busy with passengers going to Massawa, Tessenai, Agordat and Barentu. I found a bus and I went to a seat at the back. I took a deep breath and hoped that the person who sits with me be an old person who don't talk. It is not only that I have always been fond of silence and quietness but on this particular journey, the quieter I am, the safer. One of the greatest accomplishments of the current regime is the implant of spies on every little step of our way. One wrong comment or complaint about the regime or its leaders could get anyone in trouble. Everyone knows that. And the universe sent me a rather older soldier in military clothing. I didn't hate him because his face and pale skin showed that he is just an ordinary soldier whose life was flushing in front of his eyes. Am I been judgmental? I understand except when we get to talk after an hour of journey, he was complaining about the life. They often complain but they barely leave even though they know they know the border paths and a whole lot more. If there was one thing I was dead sure on doing, it was for me to never complain and suggest to him to ditch the army. Even though it was an honest opinion shared by many, it still remains a dangerous thing to say in Eritrea.

The bus was a little late than the normal hours busses to Barentu start. The journey was mostly quiet and peaceful. That peace was briefly distorted when we were just leaving the city of Keren, 91km away from Asmara, and the bus was forced to stop at a security check point. I bet the soldier sitting next to me have felt my heart beat faster and stronger because I was told there is no security checkpoint all the way to Barentu. The position of my seat didn't help since it was at the back and it appears as though I wanted to hide.

A young boy in military entered the bus and almost didn't ask anyone for travel documents. But he stopped when he reached my seat and asked me for my ID. I had employee ID card of Orotta Medical School and I gave it to him along with my national ID card. He looked at my national ID, which is the only Tigrinya one he can read and learned that I am from Asmara. And he looked at me with scary eyes and said "You are from Central Zone. Why are you going to the Gash Barka zone?" I didn't have a ready answer but I was well aware that if I don't answer immediately, he will suspect. So, I told the first lie that came to my mind with full confidence: "My sister has opened tea shop in Barentu and I want to visit her". He didn't buy it. "Get out", the order came and I left my seat and went out of the bus. A young Muslim girl of about 13 from Southern Zone came out with me, followed by her father who wanted to stand on her behalf.

As we stepped out of the bus, he began calling "Wedi keshi". Another solider came out with a cigarette between his lips. The solider told Wedi keshi "This one is from Asmara; the girl is from Southern Zone and have no ID". I was terrified but hid it well inside my skin. My biggest fear at that moment wasn't only why I was there but if I can defend my previous answer. They can ask about the sister I lied about and be in trouble. To my relief, Wedi Keshi didn't even bother to look at our IDs and gave us our cards back immediately.

Months later, when I arrived to Hashferay Prison, I learned Wedi Keshi is one of the most heartless security agents at the security checkpoint who shows no mercy.

That was a relief. But it raised questions in my head. Why did the smugglers assure me there was no security check point? The soldier told me it's been there since New Year. I didn't want to ask the soldier if there are more security checkpoints because it would be obvious I am onto something. I knew the next big towns Agordat and Barentu could have security check points. They were still far and I took the time to go through reasons to give in case the question repeats itself again. I wasn't entirely mad at Bereket because I was sure he told me what the smugglers told him. But I regretted for not asking why not Saturday? Saturday is a good cover up because it is a market day and many do travel from there to there.

But there were no more check points. At 11:20am, we reached the entry of Barentu and I miss called Bereket to tell him I will be at the bus stop in few minutes. In no more than 15 minutes, the bus stopped at the main bus station and I got off the bus to the windy and hot air of Barentu. There were many people in unordered queues to board on busses. It was my first time to step my feet in Barentu and I was surprised that there was nothing city or town about it. I looked around to find a shade in the bus station because Bereket told me the smugglers will come to pick me up from there. I sat down at a shade made by roof of a kiosk shop and miss called Bereket once again. I waited and there was no call from him or any other person. I have heard many times how smugglers work on their own timetable and don't care about us, the escapees. I was well aware of the fact that it is my money that matters to them, not my well-being and if they don't get the money from me, they can get it from the next escapee. But still I wasn't worried. I trusted Bereket a lot and I was very sure he would never hook me up with bad smugglers.

Thirty minutes passed and no-one called. I began to look around me for distraction. There were no soldiers, at least as much as I expected. I knew a lot about Barentu through word of mouth from my friend Henok who was stationed there for quite some time. He did tell me how it is infected with spies of all kinds and been a guest; I could fall into their suspicion. There was no much to do except wait while playing games on my mobile.

At 2pm, I decided to call Bereket and he accepted the call. He was saying "Hi, who are you?" I was surprised that he didn't recognize my number. And I was shocked when he said "Sammy? Sammy Andom? Asmara?" And I said "Yes, Sammy. You told me to come and I am there". I was trying to code our conversation to avoid danger but he didn't seem to get it. "Come where?" And I replied him, rather angrily, "Barentu man". Bereket was shocked. "Oh my God, I completely forgot you Sammy! Be at the bus stop. I will call them and they will come to pick you up now." He hanged up the phone with my eyes and mouth wide open.

Forgot me?! He very well knew the dangers and the risks and how they increase in Barentu, which have a heavy security presence and a place I have no reason to be in. His response kept on replying in my ears and I knew things could go wrong and therefore, I have to find a cheap motel to stay inside. But I decided to wait for him. There was no call until three. I miss called him and he called me back to say "They didn't pick you up or call you?" It felt more like a game and I was disappointed I became yet another victim of smugglers.

The next few calls I made to Bereket went unanswered or unclear. At that time, I called my trusted pal in Asmara to try to call Bereket since telephone isn't smooth outside Asmara. He called me back to say he didn't get through to Bereket. Then at 4:30 I called Henok, to tell him what was going on and he said "At 5, they will clear you out of the bus stop. Either be back to Keren and spend the night there and come home or reserve a room at a motel now. It is full of soldiers after 6pm". I called Bereket to tell him that I was really tired and frustrated of what they are doing. And he said "they are coming".

Around 5:30pm, the people at the bus stop began to leave and I began to lose hope with the smugglers. And so I went to a nearby motel and registered with my national ID to spend the night there. If the smugglers call me, I would just leave.

The motel was just patio where all the beds lied next to each other. That was a common practice since it is a hot place. The bed was full of bed bugs but I was too tired and upset to consider them enemies at that moment. I lay down on the bed and began staring at my mobile endlessly.

They ditched me. I am dumped. I began repeating those words inside my mind. There was little hope left in me because I reasoned they might want to exploit darkness.

At that moment, a soldier took the bed next to me and he began engaging me in a conversation. I was not in the mood to converse nor forgot I still have to be wary of the words I utter. I told him honestly "I wish I could chat with you now. But I am really exhausted and I have to go back to Asmara tomorrow". I thought it would close the conversation shortly. But he asked a follow up question "Why are you so tired? Where are you from?" There was no short answer in sight but that time, I didn't really care what he will think of the answer that popped up to my head. "I have a naughty brother and it's been two weeks since he left home. So I came from Asmara to enquire at Prima Country prison if they may have arrested him when somehow but he is not there". The soldier didn't seem surprised or sympathetic to the lie I told him and replied in casual voice "this cruel country...just forces everyone to be lost". After that I covered my head inside the bed sheet and pretended to be asleep. But still I was looking at my mobile. Waiting.

I waited for the call until mid-night with all I had. I was fighting my sleep until it finally defeated me. And my mobile was powering down and Barentu had no power after 11pm at that time. And to make things worse, mobile connection was off too.

I woke up at 5am the next morning and left the motel to go to the bus stop. I put myself in the already long queue to Asmara. There were no busses at all but there were many passengers. By that time, I had given up upon the smugglers and don't want to spend the day in Barentu. After about thirty minutes, I went to a small tea place and ordered tea while charging my mobile.

The busses had started taking passengers pack by pack. But still I wasn't close. So I decided if the smugglers didn't call or come by the time my turn to step on bus comes, I will be back to Asmara.

At 11:00am, a bus known by setayo came up and they were screaming at the top of their lung "Asmara, Asmara". I stepped in and I began leaving Barentu with so much anger in my heart and accomplishing nothing at all.

The journey back home was calm. I wasn't worried about the security check point of Keren this time since I was going to my home town. And they didn't even stop busses going to Asmara either. I arrived home at 4:30 and slept until 8pm.

After I woke up, the first thing I did was going to the nearest internet café to scream at Bereket. It was as though he was waiting for me online because just as a signed in to yahoo messenger; he said "Hey lost man". I was surprised at the way he greeted me and angry at how light he took the whole matter. "What happened? Why did you guys ditch me?" "I am sorry Sammy, I forgot you were coming" he replied shortly. I didn't know what to make of what he said. An escape plan, a mission that could lead to prison, disability or death was forgotten. I was really mad but handled it calmly. I said "Ok, no problem" and signed out without so much of a good bye. At 8pm, I got a call and when I answered, he said "Where are you! I am Bereket". I knew it was the smuggler for the number was Eritrea's mobile phone number. I wasn't confused about who was calling but pretended to be someone else too. At that moment, I was trying hard not to be upset with Bereket because even though he didn't care as much as I expected him to, he has always been and still is a great person. He have said good thing about the smuggler, that he knows him well in Asmara so acting rude to the smuggler wouldn't be good news to Bereket. I hanged up the phone but got a call from Bereket. "They are saying they can wait for you for tomorrow evening. Can you leave tomorrow?"

But seeing how I narrowly escaped the security check point in Keren and how I still have no guarantee when I arrive to Barentu, I declined the offer. A little while the smuggler called again and really screamed. "You ditched us! We got a job to do, we can't wait!" This time, it was plain rude and I had to reply. "You ditched me yesterday and today until lunch time! You didn't tell me to stay there or what to do and now you are blaming me!" The guy was very rude and shouted "will you come now or not?" I gave him a short answer "no" and that effectively ended my plan to escape to Sudan.

FIRST ATTEMPT TO ESCAPE TO ETHIOPIA

As with every escape, the first task was finding a smuggler to Ethiopia. Escaping Eritrea to anywhere is considered treason but it is worse for Ethiopia. Smugglers to Ethiopia are treated harshly than their Sudan counterparts too. At that time, people especially from Central Zone and Southern Zone were escaping to Ethiopia because that time was when human trafficking in the Eritrea-Sudan border and Sudan was at its highest. It was a part of Eritrea's history when the youth were getting sold like goats, losing precious body organs and sometimes their life in the process. Even though that didn't stop me at first, it did start to cross my mind after the first plan failed.

Ethiopia did feel a natural and fine choice. The border is very extensive but more dangerous as there is more military presence. The dangers of crossing to Ethiopia don't include human traffickers and for someone like me from Asmara, it is easier to resemble and act to the Southern Zone natives since we dress and talk the same. In the bigger cities, it is incredibly hard to differentiate a new comer just by the looks of it. In other words, mingling is a lot easier in Southern Zone than in Gash Barka zone.

The first thing I did was asking my friend Medhanie who escaped to Ethiopia how his escape was. He told me it was smooth route and still open if I want to come. He made it clear that the path requires a walk of 10 hours at least at night time and a payment of $1800. I didn't mind about the walk as long as it is safe and the smugglers are professionals. He assured me they were but Meda, been realistic and trying to free himself from taking responsibility from whatever that can happen, pointed out that smuggling people is very unpredictable, complicated and dependable on lack as much as on smart smugglers that he can't guarantee the escape will be a success. I knew the hard truth. But it felt better to be told the truth instead of bullshit promises made by smugglers and their cell members. So, I gave Meda the task of finalizing the deal for me and give me a call when it is go time.

In the meantime, my brother's friend Gideon was looking forward to leaving to Ethiopia and approached me if I have any information. I told him plainly about my plans to leave and my deal with Meda. Gideon asked if he can join me and I assured him he can without talking to Meda since I knew walk-driven escapes barely reject people to be smuggled. The more people who want to escape, the better. After all, smugglers don't risk their lives so we can escape from a dictator but to make money.

I was glad Gideon decided to join me on the trip. It felt safe to have a familiar face on such a goal. For sure, for the short period we are all together, we tend to get united and be supportive because failure of a single person to accomplish a task could be a disaster to everyone in the mission. But it is at the same thing reassuring to have at least one familiar face when walking and tiptoeing across the mountains and plains.

Within a week, Meda sent me a message in Facebook that basically said:

Hello Sami

You will be leaving very soon. Be ready. They will call you anytime within the next four days.

And we began waiting for the call to come. This time, Meda notified me quite early so I had the chance to clear out things sooner and remain free and be ready.

The call came two days later on Tuesday at 9:30am. It was from Ethiopia and the caller gave me his orders in a rather hasty tone:

You leave now to Mendefera. Here is the number of the driver. Good luck.

Driver is another code used to refer to smugglers. I called Gideon and he came within twenty minutes. We left to Mendefera at 10am.

At that time, I had stopped going to Orotta Medical School for my national service but I forged the original employee ID they have gave me to travel to cities. Gideon had a paper from College of Mai Nefhi. There were two security checkpoints on the way to Mendefera but we didn't have any concern or trouble in passing the posts. We looked just like everybody else on the bus and generally, we were ready and confident that the checkpoint guards had no reason to suspect a thing.

We got off the bus at the bus station and quickly disappeared into a nearby snack bar for breakfast. We were aware of snitches that wait by the bus station to see new faces that arrive to Mendefera so they can follow them around. I forgot the name but there was one particular person who had sent many to prison by following that tactic.

We ordered breakfast and I dialed the number given to me. It said no connection. Mendefera, just like other cities of Southern Zone, had terrible phone service. I tried several times to no avail. Gideon, been a devout Christian, was very calm and was telling me actions follow words. I was very pissed and worried they might leave without us. At 1PM, a call came from abroad again and I said in hurried voice "We have been here for more than an hour. We can't find him" He replied in casual voice "Don't worry. He has turned off his phone. Spend the day somewhere until 5 or 5:30. Then you call him. It is for security reason".

Even though Mendefera is a lot more secure and easier to spend a day in, I wasn't particularly excited with the instructions. It is quite impractical to expect perfect service or care from smugglers and so, we weren't surprised. I was grateful Gideon was with me because he was really calm and hopeful. We never had anything in common but I find his Christian life reassuring and comforting that day. Moreover, we were in the middle of a zone known for its cooperation and support. It is why we stayed further from the bus station but toured the rest of the city with our head held high. Around 4PM, Gideon suggested we stop by a catholic church. Later on I come to learn churches are risky to hide in as snitches target them. Around 5:30, we left the church and came back to the city. We were prepared not to be left out because we were not close to the bus stop. Sure enough at 6pm, a call came from abroad gain and he gave us a simple order: "Go to Gabir Dera Anto. He is waiting for you there." Gabir Dera Anto is a religious healing waterfall found a few kilometers out of Mendefera. We raced down to the station of minibuses that go to Gabir Dera Anto. Luckily, there was one last minibus that traveled to a village before Dera Anto. We got off the minibus around 6:30 and asked a rather old man to show us the direction Dera Anto.

The old man did look suspicious of us. It was obvious we weren't heading to Dera Anto to be healed in its waters because we didn't have any bag with us. We looked fit and in a hurry. But he didn't care to ask anything and showed us the road clearly.

The sun was going down and we weren't sure of the area. Between the village and Dera Anto, the land was plain naked with no sight of houses or settlers. One does expect wild animals in such a place but they were the least of our worries. We were just concerned about surprise soldiers but there was no sight of military tent or hat, like the ones a person sees almost in any corner of the country.

We began to walk in a hurry then slow down. If we run, we risk been suspected. Gladly, we didn't encounter anything all the way and arrived to Dera Anto after about an hour in almost pure darkness. As we took a narrow path, we started to see light from mobile phones of people on each side of the path. First, we encountered an old man on the left side of the path with a walking stick in a white garment with two girls of about 14-15. The girls had a small back-bag, which is an obvious sign of a planned escape. On the right side, we saw a young man sitting down on a stone, staring hard at his mobile. Gideon touched me and whispered "They will all go with us".

I was surprised at the parade-style display, given the risk of escaping to Ethiopia. There was no element of blending in with the religious settlers of the holy place at all. In fact, those who come to be healed were in their houses and were very quiet, with the exception of a woman who was screaming and singing at the top of her voice from somewhere.

Another thing that surprised me was at the number of people a single smuggler was willing to take. It was simply too many. At that point I wonder if they were told the truth that the escape will be on foot totally. As we stopped in one spot on the left side of the path, I looked back at the young girls with the old man, who by the way was there to make sure they leave. As though I am expert in the field, I concluded there is no way they are told the truth they will be walking from here to Ethiopia. Plus, lying is one of the most effective tools of many, if not all, smugglers.

It was 7:30 and I began dialing his number again. There was no phone line connection. This time, I was so pissed to the point I cursed in front of Gideon. To this day, I get surprised at how much calm he is as a person. After a few minutes I told Gideon we should go to a nearby hill and try.

After we reached the top of the hill and began dialing, I saw a girl and boy on the other side of the hill. At some point, the girl came close and asked me to try her number if my signal is strong. I said "I can try" and she gave me the number. It was the number of the smuggler and just like all my calls, it failed.

As we stood there doing nothing but looking at the empty screens of our phones, a hasty and tough sound came from the right side of the hill. "Who are you? Who are you?"

The girl and the boy as well as Gideon went down the hill almost instantly. I remained calm and turned my attention to the direction the voice came from with confidence. As I got closer, I saw the man was a priest with a young boy with him. I greeted them and continued "We just arrived now and we just wanted to let our families know we arrived safely." "Ok, ok my son. Go to sleep soon" he replied and continued his way.

True, the ending would have been completely different if the man was one of the so-called public soldiers. But I am sure too things would have been different if none of us stopped to talk the priest.

With little hope left, we walked back and sat down after a couple of young men. At exactly 8:00PM, the smuggler accepted my phone call. I didn't hide my frustration with him at all and I said plainly "What are you doing man? I had been here for more than an hour?" My God, his reply was very dramatic and insensitive: "I run into someone in Mendefera. Just blend with the visitors in the area for the night and we will begin tomorrow." He hanged up the phone on me and I gave Gideon a "How about now?" look. The guys who heard me talk came up with phone numbers and asked me to call. It was the number of the smuggler and I simply told them "he is not coming". Soon everyone disappeared into the trees, hills and blended in.

We slept with the guys but after some minutes Gideon suggested we walk around. I followed him and he said "we can't trust anyone. Let's find our own spot away from anybody". But we didn't find spot. We spend almost the whole night wondering the village, the housing section Dera Anto. At some point, we sat down at a cemented block behind a big hall from which the scream, singing and curse of a young woman with mental disturbance was coming randomly. The main priest of the place was awake and from time to time, he was pointing his torch directly at the young woman who was at the far end of the hall, opposite from his. I interfered and said "you are just making her madder. Stop lighting the torch at her". He didn't care and said below his lips "She is mad. She is chained but we need to chain her even harder".

As he said "we", I signaled Gideon to leave. Gideon would never approve such a thing given his born-again Christian life and I was not comfortable to chaining a young woman who has lost her mind. Noticing our move, the priest ordered us to call a man who was sleeping at the back of his hall on room number three. He wanted us to come back with him but instead, we just called and before they open the door, we disappeared from the sight.

We returned back the narrow path and sat down under a tree closer to the entrance of the village. We chose to do so because we wanted to walk back to Mendefera before anyone woke up at 5.

It was a rather long night. The fear of been found by soldiers was gone. We were just thinking on how we would spend the whole day the next day. I told Gideon I will go back home and return around 3 or 4. Gideon suggested we stay in Mendefera but I rejected because I didn't know what to do the whole day. We stayed quite for the rest of the time, with our hands deep in our pockets because it was getting really cold.

After a sleepless night, we started walking back to Mendefera at 5:00. We weren't talking at all, immersed in our own thoughts. We arrived around 7 to Mendefera and I boarded on a bus to Asmara while Gideon stayed in Mendefera.

At 3 in the afternoon, I returned back to Mendefera and we met with Gideon near the bus stop again. He told me he spent a great day with a girl he knows very well and I know a little. We began calling the number to no avail, as expected. At that time, I was having doubts about the smuggler and his network. In fact, I only came back because of Gideon and Meda. My dissatisfaction was clear on my eyes and voice that Gideon even noticed and began to fill me up with hope and positive thinking. While I applaud his positivism, I wanted to tell him it is been realistic, not negative.

The number was not still working. From the night before, we learned the last minibus to the village before Dera Anto leaves at 5:30. But we weren't sure if we have to leave or wait for a call. At that time, I went to the internet café and asked Meda we are again stuck in Mendefera. Sadly, he wasn't online to give me any kind of reply.

Around 7, the smuggler answered the phone and whispered in a really low voice "See the hill on the right. Climb up there". He hanged up the phone immediately and turned it off.

I knew immediately he was talking about Dera Anto. It was too late to go to Dera Anto and we knew we were left behind. This time, we went to the girl we both know and spent the night with her. We left at 6 before she woke up and had a quite trip back to Asmara.

I never told Gideon but the guy from abroad has called me when we were on the bus returning to Asmara. But I was so mad and at the same time lost my faith in the smugglers and rejected his call. Later Meda told me around 40 people signed up for the smuggler that he left with around half and the second call was to tell me to join the second half.

Here is the way the smuggler works: he has agents like Meda in Ethiopia and other countries who bring him people to be smuggled. They don't know each other and they simply sign up any person they find. The smuggler doesn't have any idea how many people have signed up. So that evening, once he got around 20, he just said "enough" and left. His colleague was to take the remaining once the next day.

It was quite a drama. Everyone involved knows perfectly the prison waiting if caught when escaping Eritrea. With professional smugglers like ones who smuggled my brother to Sudan, the ratio of making it successfully is really high. They are concerned about their safety and take the necessary steps, which makes it a well-planned trip. The other kinds of smugglers are concerned with cash only. Their formula is: it is a 50-50 trip. If we make it, we make a lot of money. If not, we lose it. These types of smugglers are easy to detect because all they ever talk about is money.

And that concluded my first attempt to crossing to Ethiopia. I later heard they crossed successfully.

SECOND ATTEMPT TO ESCAPE TO ETHIOPIA

Determined to cross to Ethiopia, I approached a close friend and relative of the family named Oche. He was active army personnel who joined the national service with the first round of trainees in 1994. He assured me he will get me smugglers whose route is through Senafe but should wait in patience. There were lots of promises that time that all nail down to an impressive deal of traveling to Senafe on car and the walking time wouldn't exceed an hour. One thing that I asked was that the route is through Southern Zone and he guaranteed me it is.

I never knew Oche before that. It was a family connection dot that led me to him since his army post was in the Southern Zone. He was extremely social, laud, fun and frankly kind guy. There was no single doubt in my mind regarding his promises. Looking back now, I feel that was my mistake. Doubts and questions reveal new insights into matters at hand. But I poured my heart and my mind on his hands that even though I didn't know him personally, I trusted him 100%.

On April 28, Oche called to invite me for a meeting with the smuggler. I found it strange because smugglers prefer to meet right on the last minute when the escape starts. Anyway, I told him I was working on something important and he can just talk with him and finalize things for me. Besides, I never understood why I was needed to meet smugglers before departure day. Even though that was rooted from my unshaken faith in him, it was one of the mistakes I did. Because if I had gone to that meeting, I would have learned that the escape route is through Gash Barka region and possibly decline it. Secondly, it would have given me a wonderful opportunity to actually evaluate the smuggler from his demands and the way he talks. So Oche took only Abraham to meet the smuggler.

Oche called again at 7pm to say the 30th is go time. I was really excited and wrapped up the work I was doing. But not long after, he called again to say the date has been changed due to "unexpected circumstances".

Though I was confident in the route Oche brought, I was not completely at ease because the unholy month of May was entering. For those of you who don't know, May 24 is the so-called "Independence Day", which is supposed to make the month a happy one. But it brings with it frustration and discomfort because of the heavy military presence on every corner, who ask for identification paper and travel document on every step. Every youth remembers May as a hell-month for it completely strips away even the tiniest freedom we have somehow.

It would have been easier if I wasn't walking around on a forged travel document. It is not hard to imagine the trouble and suspicion one goes through traveling to any border of the country, when one can't walk freely on his neighborhood for the whole month. However, all my questions can only be answered and addressed by the smuggler, who normally knows the situation of security check points and border movements. And I got the answers on April 30 when Oche came to spend the night in my home as I was to leave on May 1.

The first thing he did was giving me and my nephew Abraham bus tickets. The ticket said "Asmara – Barentu", a town in Gash Barka zone. My primary worry was about the possible heavy security checkpoints to any city of the country. Now the security checkpoint of Keren, which is heavy and tight throughout the year, came to my mind. I didn't let it bother me for I believed he must have an explanation for the change from Southern Zone to Gash Barka zone.

Sadly, Oche was heavily drunk and repeating the same thing over and over again. Every time I open my mouth, he would say "Sami, Sami...stop!" and go on repeating the same things. I feel silly remembering that night. Really foolish. Because the fact that he came drunk when we were supposed to have a talk about a live-or-die mission was a pure signal how light he took the matter. Anyway, his repetitive words could be summed up as follows:

"We changed the date because of travel documents. We thought of using travel documents issued by the Ministry of Defense to its soldiers. But it was risky because soldiers come home in May and so traveling to the border around May 24 with travel document of MoD is highly dangerous. Now we have made you a new document that can let you travel to any part of the country with your head held high. No security checkpoint will bother you. The smuggler will give you the travel documents tomorrow May 1. If you don't leave tomorrow, you will be forced to leave after May 24. Because a national security agent has confirmed to us that they are tipped about 'disturbers' who plan to enter from Sudan and Ethiopia."

"Now you will take Barentu bus but get off in Keren. Then you go to Hagaz. Then you will take bus to Agordat and again another bus to Barentu. Then from Barentu, you will go straight to Shambko. In Shambko, he will leave you hidden in one room. Then he will come back dressed completely as a farmer. And around 8pm, you will begin your journey and walk for no more than two hours. He knows the route very, very well so there is no need to be afraid."

Almost after each paragraph, Oche was saying with so much emotion: "I have seen many worse things in my life. But I have never been terrified like today". That alone was a big hint for me about his in confidence in the process or the smuggler. He was very much terrified to the point his fear was in fact transferred to me. But I didn't act on it.

I had many questions for Oche that evening but what's the point of asking a drunken man? The main question I had was why change busses if the travel document is strong enough to open the door for me to travel to any part of the country? I didn't get why the smuggler get to look like a farmer while we still will look like the city boys we have always been.

That evening alone could have hinted me their plan had an obvious flow. I didn't know what hindered me from backing out or dumping them. Around mid-night I called someone (who shall remain nameless for security for he still lives in Eritrea) to tell him how the escape plan don't make sense. He knows Oche more than me and assured me he is a credible guy who knows what he is doing. I guess the fact the person in charge was Oche made it hard for me to back out or complain as he was family member trusted by everybody else but me.

The next morning on May 1, we woke up and left together with Oche and Abraham to the bus station. On the way, around Martin Luther School, Oche stopped to greet someone dressed in completely black outfit, including his hat. Later he told me that he is the guy who got us the travel documents. I ignored him and walked to the bus station in complete silence. I wonder if he got my message of dissatisfaction and doubt through my stunned silence.

We arrived at the busy bus stop and met the smuggler. His name is Rezene Weldesalasie and as I later discovered, he is from the town Dibarwa. Rezene is a muscular and strong looking man in his mid-forties with a noticeable lost tooth and bald hair. He was wearing plastic shoes typically known as Congo or Shida (famous with army people). After they greeted each other, Rezene and Oche led us to a nearby snack bar where we had hot tea. After a minute, Rezene stood up to go to the bath room and Oche soon followed him.

Oche came back and handed me over an A4 paper and said "you show this along with your national ID card, no one will dare to ask you". I opened it and regretted paying 7,500.00nfa each for that paper I very well know and could have forged myself. I had templates of such documents which I got from a friend in case something came up. The forged document basically stated I went to military training with the 23rd round and was doing my national service at a construction company named Badme (owned by the MoD) and that I was demobilized from the army due to health reasons. Abraham's said he is 25th round and was demobilized from construction company Ali Musa. Both documents had stamps and were signed by Colonel Haile, which could be real or fake. I felt cheated and lied to. The doubts and fears I had increased dramatically. Normally, I am a stubborn person and I do things I only believed in and accepted. Since I was well familiar with the paper, I knew its limits. I knew Oche and the smuggler were lying about its powers. Yet, I just took it and stayed quite. I like to believe it is out of respect for Oche but it is something I can't explain.

And that paper presented us with unbelievable amount of trouble and agony.

After that, we headed to the bus and Oche told Abraham to sit on the front, Rezene in the center section and me at the back section of the bus. I said thanks to Oche and departed. The reason they didn't chose Keren bus was because Barentu busses begin at least an hour before Keren busses do and the Keren security checkpoint isn't active before 8-9am. Of course, that's their theory.

We arrived to Keren around 8 and we got off at the bus stop. Then to my surprise, Rezene approached me and said "I will look if the security checkpoint is up and running. When I call you, you board on a minibus to Hagaz and we continue". I still didn't see the application of the travel document and it was a further proof of their lies.

I was very familiar with Keren and so, I took Abraham to a good restaurant and we ate a nice breakfast. Then we called Oche to tell him we are in Keren. After around 30 minutes, Rezene called to say "it is safe. Come". We boarded on a minibus to Hagaz but after a few minutes he called again to say "get out of the minibus". We did as we were ordered and I called Rezene to ask him what's going on. He told me to walk to Keren Laelay, specifically a shop called "Bekit". I knew the shop from before and so went there without any problem. Rezene was waiting by a corner near the shop and approached me with so much ease that surprised me and said "They are testing the minibuses". Then I fired the question that had been in my mind all along "Then why did you guys sell us the travel documents?" He looked to the sides and avoided the question. Then he looked at me and said "How about we pass the checkpoint by walking around it through the village of Begu?" I looked at him with my mouth open. How on earth Rezene, a so-called professional smuggler, asked me for such a tip was a total surprise. I asked him back once again with a rather strong tone "Didn't you guys tell us you have done a thorough study of the route? How do you expect me to know which route is safe?" I continued "But it seems like you are not sure at all. We can return from here before it is too late". Again, he skipped the question and started crossing to the other side while talking "No, no, Samuel. It is just for extra safety." We followed him like a couple of goats.

And that was another mistake I made. The confusion, doubt and obvious in-confidence of Rezene were the biggest signal of their weak and poor plan. I blame myself to this day for the times we spent on prison because there was no clearer message about the unprofessionalism of Rezene as a smuggler and how they had no idea about the journey ahead.

Rezene stopped a minibus heading to Hagaz and whispered "we will see our chances" and stepped into the minibus. And luckily, luck was on our side. The minibus wasn't stopped for checkup.

Once we got off in Hagaz, Rezene boasted about his skills. "You see, if you are confident, nothing can get in the way. Nothing." It was clear he was trying to gain my confidence and approval. So far, according to my balance, his skills were well below zero. I am sure until know that he had in fact understood that I know me and Abraham were in a middle of a messy escape plan that could lead us to bitter times, including death.

And here is something that I didn't understand about Rezene. I know the risk I was taking to be smuggled out of the country. And he very well knew the even bigger and dangerous risk he is taking when smuggling people out of the country. He didn't seem to have cared a little bit. Just like I was not comfortable to be smuggled by someone who seems to have no idea of the way to the border, he should have been uncomfortable and warned to smuggle someone whose eyes were getting incredibly worried and sad.

We didn't stay long in Hagaz. It was very hot and seemed pretty much dead. As we were walking its streets, Rezene pointed to some mountains on the right side of the town and side "this is Hashferay, a Para-commando military training site for all defense forces."

I wonder why he didn't mention that it is also prison. In fact, Hashferay is very well known for been a prison in the community more than a training camp. We left Hagaz to Agordat, without even having the slightest idea that it was to be the place I would be jailed for a year.

There was nothing unique or interesting on the journey from Hagaz to Barentu. We stopped in the hot town of Agordat but continued to Barentu instantly. The only thing remarkable that had happened was a call that came to Rezene. He told me it is the guy who made the travel documents and who Oche stopped to greet early in the morning when we were on our way to the bus station. Once again, I ignored Rezene.

My ignorance wasn't emerging only from the dissatisfaction of how the operation was been carried out but from exhaustion. Moving from bus to bus and realizing what Oche told me differed from what had happened so far exhausted me and frankly, scared me. I generally avoided looking at Rezene directly but in the few times I had a quick side-look, I was questioning him in my head and he was failing.

We arrived to Barentu, the town I never wanted and thought to set foot again, at 4:30pm. I thanked God and took a deep breath of satisfaction. Even though we were in a place known for its dense military and security presence, I felt closer to leaving the hell-hole country I lived in for nearly thirty years. Rezene quickly went on to check the busses and came back to lead us to a restaurant in the bus stop. He ordered a peanut based snack called "ful" and came back. Upon sitting down, Abraham surprised us both by asking him "what shall we say should things go wrong?" Rezene was not pleased with the question. "What wrong! We are done now! Nothing will go wrong". He stood up from his chair just as quick as he sat down. Then he left to the tab water. It was an obvious move to ignore further questions because he had washed his hands when we just came in, literary 5 minutes earlier.

I took the chance to share with Abraham what I think should happen. "Let's just protect Oche. We say everything was finalized for us from abroad. We know nothing".

Let me fast-forward you to my prison time in Hashferay. Sometime in February 2014, a prisoner named Solomon told me the reason he got caught when going to Ethiopia was because he had negative thought of what to say if been captured, how to react and what to do. He was implying the power of positive thinking could have made a positive difference.

While I generally accept the power of positive thinking, I also believe been realistic is stronger and important. Rezene made errors not because of my doubts because I got those doubts from his actions and shortcomings in the first place. I am sure now if he had done a terrific job, leaving no doubt in my mind but still failed, I would have simply called it fate.

And the ignorance of Abraham's question by Rezene was to have a serious consequence. That question was also a question I wanted to ask Oche the previous night but he gave me no chance to speak.

At 5:10, we boarded an old bus to go to the final town in our journey from Eritrea to Ethiopia: Shambko. Rezene told me it is around two hours away. The bus was overloaded with people and goods. It was obvious there is no traffic control. The road was full of red dust that made its way into the bus through the broken windows and holes on the floor of the bus.

After about an hour, the town began to appear. It appeared smaller than I thought. But my mind crossed to the series of mountains at the back of the town. They were the fence that separate Eritrea and Ethiopia. Crossing the mountains means been free. It seemed closer and I got more relaxed.

Sadly, the relaxation was short-lived. Unexpectedly, Rezene told the driver to stop the bus and we got off. The town was still around 40 minutes away and we got off to a more or less empty land. That wasn't what Oche told us the night before.

I asked Rezene: "Oche told me we are to board off the bus at the center of the town"

"This time entering the center is dangerous because security forces wonder the town now. But don't worry. You see those mountains in front of us? It is Ethiopia. It is an hour away."

His answer was troubling not because it wasn't anything like Oche told us but that the sun was not yet set and crossing during broad sunlight was unheard of and dangerous. The land between us and the mountains was plain that a hiding place was not insight. But I let him take control and didn't ask.

After five minute, we saw two men coming towards us normally. One was dressed in military while the other was in civilian clothing. It was obvious they were walking around yet the shorter man in the military clothing had his eyes fixed on us. As we passed them along, Rezene told me the truth that he is frustrated with the look of the guy.

I didn't have a reply. I wasn't able to even fake words of strength. Rezene took a deep breath and began talking "If they look at you, just stare at them hard. This is your country. Held your chest high and walk straight. You are free to walk around".

I laughed internally. If I was free, why am I going through this Rezene? Why am I paying you $2000.00? Isn't it because I was an unofficial prisoner in a country dimmed liberated? It would be unfair to judge his smuggling career based upon my less than 24 hours with him because he had said he had smuggled at least one boy a few weeks ago. Either to show his disappointment with me and Abraham for his own reason or to encourage us, he was repeating about a guy he had smuggled before us: "Amanuel was the best guy I had to smuggle. He was really great. He asks no questions. He simply follows me". It could be pure lie or the truth. Based upon my experience with him, I can only say now that lady luck must have been with him in the past.

His statement was to be tested just ten minutes later.

Suddenly, we heard a hard voice coming from the back. "Hey, stop! Stop!" We looked back and three soldiers come running towards us. I noticed an open door to a rather old house and figured they came from it. They greeted us warmly and said "You seem to be guests. Do you have travel documents?" We gave them. It was then I saw Rezene's travel document was exactly like mine. I wondered, instantly, if I had paid for his document too. Because normally one travel document costs 5000.00nfa and I paid 15000 apparently for me and Abraham. Even though I felt tricked, it was not my concern at all at the moment.

The soldiers asked the expected question "What did you come here for?" I and Abraham kept quiet. Rezene told them we came to dig gold. I learned for the first time about the availability of gold in the mountains of Shambko. "We know the place very well. You can ask people here too. They know us". I knew Rezene indeed knew the place somehow because two of the soldiers had greeted him with his first name. That time I moved back a bit to pee in ditch there and saw additional four soldiers were at the back with their guns.

I knew we were in trouble. I knew they knew, too.

The soldiers passed the travel documents from one to another. Then the tallest soldier with eyeglasses started talking pointing and looking at me: "You are telling me he came to dig gold?! Let's just go"

And we began following one soldier on the front and the rest of the soldiers on our sides and back to the house they came from. The house was fenced with thorns. In the center was a big tree. There was a young man under the tree with a soldier guarding him. Other than that, there was nothing to see.

Two of the soldiers who accompanied us went into the rooms while we sat down on the ground. Then Rezene wrote slowly on the ground "Gold".

It seemed too late to tell us what to say now. All we knew now is we came for Gold. The hardest question will come and I was busy trying to make up good reasons. The difficult thing was I didn't know how both Rezene and Abraham will answer any questions asked. Because a difference in answers to the same or similar question is an obvious red flag that the interrogators will use to justify their ideas.

One of the youngest soldiers, about 17 years old, seems to have seen Rezene's writing movement on the ground. He came close and told us to sit far away from each other and take off our shoes. Within a few minutes, Rezene was called into one of the rooms. He was there for less than five minutes and I was called.

The room was very small, about 3 by 3. It was dark with only a single, tiny room open and had one bed on side and an old wooden box on the other side. The interrogator, who was an old, thin man in military clothing and one of the soldiers were seated on the bed while I sat down on a small stool in front of them. The interrogator engaged me in a dialog immediately:

Him: "What's your name?"

Me: "Kiflemariam Sium"

Him: "Why did you come to Shambko?"

Me: "To dig gold"

Him: "Dig where?"

Me: "Here in Shambko"

Him: "There is no gold in Shambko. Tell me exact village and mountain you want to dig in?"

Me: "I came here after hearing there is gold in Shambko. Rezene knows the village and location better than me"

I am not sure if I could have given a better answer. All I knew was that I shouldn't take time to answer the question. The answer I gave seemed the best in my view because it gave Rezene, the only one who knows the place, a flexible chance to select a safe village and mountain. The responsibility was falling on Rezene's back because I felt by not giving answers or giving very short answers, he can create a story of some kind that would be believable.

Him: "So, it means you are familiar with the gold business?"

Me: "No, it is my first time"

Him: "Why do you want to join the business then?"

Me: "Because I heard it is profitable"

And then he asked me the question I was not able to answer. Since the second they stopped us, I had looked away for a credible and sensible way to answer it. I knew I was going to be asked but I didn't know what to answer.

Him: "Ok Kiflemariam. Where do you know Rezene?"

I replied right away "I know him just like anybody else I know in Asmara."

Him: "Ok good. Is there anyone in Shambko who can bail you out?"

Me: "No"

Him: "Can Rezene bail you?"

Me: "Ask him"

He sent me out and called Abraham. Abraham stayed there the longest. It was troubling. I imagined that they bombarded him with questions based upon what I and Rezene had said. After fifteen minutes, Abraham came out followed by the interrogator, who ordered one of the soldiers to bring rope and tie us up. The soldiers led us towards the tree.

And I got to be tied up in a style called "helicopter", except we didn't hang down from a tree branch. It is very famous in the army of Eritrea and very hurtful, which is roughly illustrated below. The arms and feet as well as the neck hurt a lot. And the gravels and thorns on the ground almost penetrated our chest. I asked the soldier if he could loosen up the rope around my arm thighs. He was too afraid to do so. Then they took Rezene a bit far and chained him the same way. We continued that way for two and half hours.

© HornAffairs.com: the popular system of torture - helicopter

My legs felt numb while my arms seemed to be unbolting from my body. The soldier in front of me was avoiding looking at my eyes directly. He knew it was hard but can't do anything about it. You see, we were all forced to go through what we go through.

At the moment, none of us have admitted of our intention of crossing to Ethiopia. Alone in my world, I was thinking how I can keep on playing the game of denial. There were only two options: admit or keep the gold story. Changing stories only leads to admitting the truth. It was bad enough that three of us have no idea what each of us were saying and thinking separately. It was easy to understand that our answers can't be the same at all. That made me hopeless.

In the darkness, they called Abraham again and took him for further questioning. Again, they brought him out and took me in. My arms and legs felt relaxed. I felt really free to be free of the chains. But still they chained both my hands from the back around my thigh and led me to the room. As I and Abraham passed along opposite directions, he moved his lips to say "I admitted".

It was such a huge relief for me. There was no way we can keep on lying without having any basis of the area or the plan. Admitting the truth takes away a lot of load from us. But it also meant unloading many years of imprisonment on Rezene.

Upon my return to the room, the only window was closed and the room was completely dark. The interrogator had pointed his tiny torch to the small table between his bed and my stool. I wasn't able to see their face this time. I knew there was someone with him but can't tell who in the darkness. However, I can see clearly a big whip on the table.

I wasn't surprised. I know the army and security agents use flogging as a means of torture to get more information. The room was darker so one wouldn't identify the name of the person doing the beating.

The interrogator started talking in the complete darkness. His tone and voice was as calm and smooth as a preacher: "Ok Kiflemariam. Now it is all over. We know you intended to escape the country by crossing the border. Your partner has told me the whole truth. It is typical. Some of you escape successfully, some of you are caught. It is cycle of life. The smartest thing to do now is learn from your mistakes because you have a merciful, not a killer government."

"I was running away to Ethiopia".

Him: "Who was taking you to Ethiopia?"

Me: "I was going away with Rezene"

Him: "Where did you meet him?"

Me: "A friend in US just told me to meet him at the bus stop this morning. The deal was finalized from abroad for me through the internet"

The interrogator couldn't take the question further. The fact is they have no internet access to check my messages for confirmation.

On return, they laid me over on the ground with my arms tied so close but my legs stretched freely. Still my chest was in pain from the thorns and gravels on the ground. And with that, I tasted the bitter punishment I used to hear and read about all my adult life.

A few minutes later, they took Rezene to the test room. I doubt they asked him more than one question because I heard them beating the crap out of him in the silent night. I put my chin on the ground and closed my eyes. I felt really bad that he had to go through it alone and alone only. I felt incredibly guilty yet I didn't know what I could have said or done to prevent the torture. I waited in silence for him to come out but it continued. In all the times he stayed there, he didn't make a single sound. And when he was coming out, he was walking as though he wasn't beaten. They took him to his side and tied him up in helicopter style.

The night was long. I wasn't able to sleep with so many ideas rushing through my mind. My arms have become numb as each second passed by. Changing sleeping position wasn't allowed, as was talking with each other. And to make things worse, it was a windy night and the dust was making its land on our faces straight. With our arms tied to the back, there was no way to clean it up off our face. There was a single guard for me and Abraham and another one for Rezene alone. The soldier in front of us was young and playing with this gun but never forgetting to keep his eyes on us.

Unexpectedly, after an hour, they began going through our pockets. A tall soldier along with two soldiers, who were obviously in their teen years, began going through me. The main soldier was obviously one of the kinds who do everything they can to go higher in rank. He was blabbing about the government, the country and betrayal. The other two soldiers were symbolically standing there, without touching me at all. In fact, they spoke only once. After he found gum in my pocket, he began removing its cover but one of the teen soldiers took it away from his hand and said "He is going through a lot. Give him back his gum" and he cut the gum in two halves and put one half in my mouth and the other half in my pocket. I had the chance to look at his face when he was doing that and my God, I read an honest and innocent sympathy in his eyes.

The check returned my mobile phone and 1300nfa. Then he found my old, green wallet. To this day, I don't understand why I took it because I barely used it even at home and that day too. He began going through it and got a piece of paper. He read it and he placed it close to my eyes for me to read. I was shocked.

It was an original travel document a guy gave me in case I wanted to cross to Sudan through Sawa Military Camp. I thought I left it behind with my other fake ID at home. I got it long ago but still it was a dangerous discovery. "What is this?" he asked me in hard tone. I knew if the paper ends up in the hands of the interrogator, things will get messier and harder for me. So I decided to give him a reason that is somehow truthful. With a beggar's eyes, I looked at him directly in the eye and told him: "A travel document I got for my escape plan to Sudan". He looked to either side and put it on my mouth. "Eat it" he said. It was the most generous gift anyone can get from security units of the government. It was especially great gift and gesture for it came from someone who had all the signs of a cruel, kiss-ass soldier. Though he was the first to capture us during the day and he was tough on us throughout our stay under their capture, I am deeply thankful for what he did to me in relation to the travel document.

In case you are wondering what the big deal is about the travel document, the government takes forged travel documents very seriously. Given its tight control and endless demands for national service, we the youth run away to cities and start leading a life on fake documents. Until the source of the document is traced back and captured, the person caught with a fake travel ID is subject to beating and torture. In many cases, they follow a policy that goes on like this: either admits you created it or get the person who created it. Been a creator is considered one of the highest crimes and the prison times and the beatings are equally high. My case was scary because the travel ID was original and its owner can be traced easily. Though I didn't know where or who the original owner is, they would try. And if they fail to get him directly through its number for any reason, they would beat me up until I get the name of the person I got it from directly, who was still in Asmara.

Then he went to Abraham and found "Xebel" (kind of a holy soil popular in Orthodox followers, believed to give protection and guidance) and started mocking us: "Asmara people believe in Priest Abune Aregawi to protect you from our radar".

They finished their search and went back to their boss with 1500 for both me and Abraham and my mobile. Then they untied me and took me to their boss. The soldier who searched me and another soldier were present in the room. The man asked me "how much money did you have?" My searcher replied for me "1000". His boss scolded him saying "why did you answer for him?!" and he turned to look at me. I assured him I had less than or 1000. Given the enormously Godly thing he did for me, I wished he had said I had 200; 100 for each me and Abraham and take the rest for himself.

Upon return, they tied me up even harder and I began moving my head from side to side out of desperation, for it was the only part of my body I was able to move. The guard noticed that and stood up from his stool and stood over me and said "why are you making many moves? Are you up to something?" I was staring at his feet for they were the only part of his body I was able to see as he was standing and I pleaded "My bro, the gravels under my chest are about to make a hole there. Clean the ground for me please." He replied quickly in a rather harsh tone, possibly to scare me off "You sleep silently now. You make one move now, you are dead!" and he returned back to his stool.

The night was over without sleeping but me and Abraham had no signs of tiredness or boredom because our mind was very much occupied by what will happen in the days to come. At that time, I had no idea about the military unit that has captured me. Looking at the very young soldiers and their lack of discipline, I did know they are part of the so-called "Public Army" unit which was controlling Eritrea by a mighty wave. While knowing the exact name of the unit wouldn't magically set us free, it could prove to be helpful if we send the name back to Asmara and someone can do something then. The truth is Eritrea is deeply corrupted country powered by 'I scratch your back, scratch mine' policy. I was sure if somebody can locate some official with close ties, directly or indirectly, to the military unit, they can even send us free without going through the lengthy process of interrogation and prison. All it takes is finding the way to a stronger man who can make the call.

That morning, we saw the soldiers cook their breakfast. It was obvious to see how poorly funded they are. They had one dish to bake then clean and cook the only kind of food they eat, lentils! They brought us on a plastic dish they made out of a 3-liter oil tank. They loosen our right hands but were tied back almost instantly because we weren't able to eat the food in front of us. The bread was over-burned, very dark while the lentil was salt less and watery.

It took me back to my military training years ten years ago. How I regret cursing the food they gave us then. It appeared the best kind of food any one can wish for when I was given a food one can't throw even at pigs.

But the soldiers were eating in a way that looked more like an eating competition. In a matter of minutes, their plate was over and everyone was washing their hands. When our plate returned to them untouched, they hurried to go at it again. I knew they are very well underpaid but I didn't know they are this hungry. Why and how they stay dedicated, capturing people who want to live the horrible life they live daily is beyond me.

Soon after, they took us out of the fenced compound, across the road into a hole to pee. We were encircled by six soldiers with their guns and one soldier said "Get in the hole and do your thing!" I looked at him in surprise and disgust. The hole was full of dry feces to the point there was no space to land a feet on. The soldier looked at me "Don't waste time. Get in!"

As an Eritrean, it wasn't the first time I had to "do my thing" in a close range with others. But this one was in an extremely narrow and filthy place. And it is really impossible "to go at it" when curious eyes are looking at you constantly from all directions.

"Can I pee standing here?" I asked him politely; afraid I might lose my privilege. Another soldier interfered and said softly "Yes. Hurry up only".

We were returned to be tied under the tree again. Then they took Rezene alone.

After that, the questioning continued. I and Abraham were called on after another and we both insisted we had no idea how the whole escape plan was arranged or who was involved. We were sure our response was making Rezene's fate darker and darker but we didn't know what else to say. At the heart of our drama was protecting Oche at all costs. I bet Rezene knew that and he knew what was waiting for him as a smuggler. It was why I later confirmed he did everything he could to push the case towards Oche in an attempt to soften the charges against him.

Rezene was called after us and came back after around 15 minutes.

Then they called Abraham who stayed the longest. When he came out of the interrogation room, Abraham left behind a question for me, a question I was hoping to never hear: "Where do you know Oche?"

Since both Rezene and Abraham were questioned before me, I had no idea who mentioned Oche first. My answer did matter because it may or may not match what was previously told by Rezene or Abraham. Not knowing what he was told, I told the interrogator that I don't know Oche and everything was cooked for me from abroad. He looked at me and the table intensely then said "Can you call your friend abroad and ask him?" I didn't weaver in my response: "No, we only communicate online".

Things were easier for me than Abraham because Abraham had met Rezene before when Oche arranged the meeting. That half an hour meeting complicated things for both of them as they had to answer tough questions why they met, who arranged it, where they met and who was present.

The interrogator kept me there for a few minutes with absolute silence. I knew he was generating questions but seemed to have none for he told me go and be tied up.

Upon return, they let me and Abraham sit close and even chat. It was a clear sign that they were done with us. Until that moment, Rezene was saying we came to dig gold and that we said we came to cross to Ethiopia because we were afraid of been tortured, like he was. I don't recall when but at some point when he got a chance Rezene had told me that he was confident we would stand the beating and torture and stand firm on our reply that we came to dig gold. While I felt sorry for failing his expectation and subjected him to unbelievable torture then and after, I still don't believe we could have kept on making stories about the gold digging business and industry we had no idea about. One can stand punishment on the ground that his story is intact and credible. For us, we didn't have the same storyline to stand our ground on.

A few minutes later they called me only and asked me a series of questions: "With whom were you planning to spend the night?", "Where did you hide your bed sheets to use in the mountains?" and so forth. They were simple questions that required no lie from us: we didn't plan to spend the night anywhere. Period. After that, they let us sit under the tree though our hands remained tied. It gave us the chance to actually have a proper conversation.

"Why did you mention Oche?" was the first question I asked Abraham.

"I didn't mention him. He asked me where I know Maakoray. I thought Oche must also be known as Maakoray to Rezene so I told him I know him in Dekemhare" Abraham replied.

I needn't ask more. At that time, the information was given and all that remains is for Oche to be hunted and brought to prison. Unless I tip him and he finds a way out of the mess, hopefully by corrupting some official as common sense dictates.

I have wholeheartedly tried to protect Oche from been caught. After his name was mentioned, I knew Command 1 wouldn't rest until they capture him. It was why I hurried to let him know the mission had failed and he needs to do something to protect himself. I have sent him at least five letters, which he all got. On his part, he tried to protect himself somehow but it failed.

When Oche arrived to Hashferay, he was spending out rumors that it was me who failed the mission; that I admitted we were going to Ethiopia first. I was hurt to hearing that but even worse was that he was talking about something private with God knows who. My closest friends in prison didn't know we were connected yet prisoners I know only in face would come to me and tell me I should have endured the questions and save all. I don't really know what kind of story Oche was feeding them but the truth of the matter is that I didn't break down first. But even if Abraham had endured, I would have let them know that we were going to Ethiopia. Oche was telling people that I have said

"I swear to God, I am going to tell the truth". I may or may not have said that but after me, Rezene was asked. He was told that I have sworn and Rezene thought I broke down first and admitted the truth. I don't blame any of them but I still smirk at their demand we should have endured the torture until the end. If I am demanded to hang down from a ceiling, then there must be a spot to hang down from. We had no story. We had nothing and what we told them before been prepared was not related at all. While I feel sorry for Oche and the enormous pain and loss he went through, I don't regret the decision I made.

Oche did make me look like a bad guy in the eyes of the prisoners he was close with but I gently ignored it all. The truth is I knew Rezene and him were subject to longer sentences and torture, thus I found it best to ignore their blames in the full hope it made them feel better. On the other hand, I found Bereket, the guy who made the fake travel documents more factual and understanding. We were close but we never mentioned our case except one day he asked me he had no idea how the security agents came directly to his house and take him out when he was watching TV with his kids. He knew I had nothing to do with his case because I was never connected to him directly at all levels. Yet, he also believed it was me who blabbed about our escape plan when we were caught, as was told by Oche.

May 2, 2013 was happy Thursday. It was rather slow day. The only thing unique that happened was we had pasta and milk for lunch. You see, the guy who we saw under the tree when we came in was a prisoner whose wife lived in Shambko. He was member of the Eritrean Police working in the port of Assab. He came to visit his wife and family in Shambko and he was caught on suspicion of been a smuggler. They had no evidence against him but a weak suspicion. In fact, they made him swear and sign that he will never smuggle people under any circumstances and for his father to guarantee that and let him go. At that time, it surprised me that can be forced to be under oath for something he may not have even thought of doing all his life. But when I arrived to Hashferay, I realized how lucky he was to have walked free

44

with a signature only.

We were under constant watch of the guards while Rezene was still tied and chained to his chest alone a few steps away from us. The soldiers were talking, non-stop, about girls and sex in a rather awful way. They had no shame that we were listening to everything even though we didn't know the girls they were talking about personally. Unless that is their way of stealing the attention of prisoners to keep them away from plotting to break free. It didn't seem to work.

Around 3pm, Abraham whispered in my ears: "I am going to jump across the thorn fence and run". It was a plan on its own but a poor one. And I am not saying that because I am lousy at running but we weren't in good place to run away from. The land was plain clear on all directions. The only residential buildings in sight were the ones at the center of town and they were at least an hour away and infested with snitches. The mountains at the border, located an hour or two hours away are hard to reach given the heavy presence of security agents. Running back to Barentu was a more or less deadly attempt for it was 2 hours away with no hills or caves in between. And to top it all, we don't know any of the ways.

But I didn't want to interfere with Abraham's plan. I looked at him and said "I am not sure if it is a good idea but I won't stop you either"

He gave it some thought and cancelled it, too. At 6pm, we were called so our testimony and words can be properly written. It was that evening that I know the unit capturing us was "Spy Unit Division 57", as it was the header of the A4 paper my testimony was been written on.

Around 7PM, I saw the soldiers taking their blanket and guns and leave the compound into the darkness. I noticed they were going in groups to different directions. Border crossing is best done at night time under the umbrella of darkness and the soldiers were going to hunt for possible escapees like us.

I felt somewhat shameful. I was caught by soldiers who were chatting and having fun time after they had dinner at 6PM and waiting for their 7PM night-watch. There was something prideful about been captured by soldier who goes out seeking to capture someone and the target taking great care not to be caught. There was a great feeling to be captured at the very border, in the mountains.

The next Friday, Good Friday, started off casually. They brought us the same kind of food for breakfast with one cup of tea for each. At 10am, four soldiers came having a bunch of ropes. I noticed the younger soldiers just wanted to watch, with a lot of love and pity in their eyes. They were standing guard, unable to do anything for us and rejecting to have a hand in the process they are required to participate.

They passed the ropes multiple times through the upper section of our arms to the back. One can't run, at least at good speed and for long period, at that speed. The interrogator came towards me and asked what I had with me. I told him "shoes, mobile and money".

They are required to transfer my shoes along with my mobile but he kept all except my mobile. I didn't mind that I am not allowed to wear shoes or belt anyway. At that time, I was sure we were going to Barentu's main prison: Prima Country. I have heard how it was usually overcrowded but is well managed compared to many prisons of the country.

Two soldiers accompanied us out. The ground was hard to walk bare foot for it was full of gravels and thorns. We were glad they didn't rush us for we can walk slow and put our legs carefully on at least thorn-free spot.

This time, we were told to stay close but never talk. Rezene was chained with iron bars (shown below, typically known as ferro) to his front. His spirit and strength were still high. He endured the heavy beatings and had no sign of pain at all.

© HornAffairs.com: Ferro Chains. Arms go into both holes and the bolts are screwed down until the iron bar reaches the bones of the arms, often opening the top skin.

I and Abraham were tied with our arms to the back in a style called "Otto" (eight).

©HornAffairs.com Otto

We were instructed to sit down at the edge of the road we have gotten off from the bus on Wednesday. And soon enough, a bus came from Shambko and it was stopped. Abraham boarded first then the shorter, firmer and merciless soldier who was present in all the interrogations then me and Rezene then the other soldier, who was rather old and quite.

All eyes on the bus were on us. We were hearing whispers like "poor kids", "their poor mothers" etc. After a few minutes, one young girl stood up and gave her seat to Abraham. Then the same thing followed for me and Rezene.

I sat down with an old woman. She began saying motherly stuff and kept on reminding me it hurts my mother more than it hurts me. There was no question about that. Except mom had no idea I was in the hands of the cruel regime. However, the person who told my family I was caught trying to cross the border was on that bus with us, sitting with Abraham who gave him phone numbers of our family. Here is the story:

His name is Yemane and he came to Hashferay one month after me. He was in Shambko to go to Ethiopia but had to return after three days for his smuggler ditched him. His smuggler has connected him with a woman to stay with and gave him the proper dress code and tips to blend in the town. But on the third day, the host was worried and told Yemane to leave. He waited until Monday to tell my family because he didn't want to ruin the Easter Sunday for them.

After that escape plan failed, he planned to go to Sudan in June and was caught and followed me to Hashferay. We remained close while we were there until the day we both left Hashferay on the same day.

Back to the bus, the soldier in the middle was looking back at me and Rezene non-stop, while the older soldier didn't even care. It seemed as though he was been forced to be on that bus too. Realizing his obvious ignorance, I turned to a girl on the back seat and gave her my brother's number so she can tell him about my capture. She tried but failed. The soldier didn't care at all that we were conversing, as long as the tough soldier on the front doesn't see.

We got off the bus at the outskirts of Barentu. Rezene, who was very familiar with the area, said "We are not going to Prima Country prison!" We began walking on the hot, thorny and rough paths of Barentu full of gravels with the following us at very close range. We were passing through the residential streets as everyone sees us. It was obvious prisoners walking on the streets in this fashion is very common because no one stopped to look at us, stared at us or showed some kind of sympathy. There were children playing on the streets and they didn't even stop to look at us for a minute. It was obvious to understand that we were just other prisoners who make it through their streets almost daily. No surprises there.

After walking for forty minutes, we saw a fenced compound full of tents with soldiers moving from there to there. They took us straight to two rooms made from bricks. They untied us and pushed three of us into the room and passed three liters of water before they locked the door firmly from the outside. And warning came: "There is no more water. Drink carefully!"

When we sat down, something fall down from Rezene and took me by surprise. His baby Nokia mobile phone!

I have no idea how he kept it hidden in Shambko when he was been searched thoroughly and how it never fell down when he was beaten head to toe. He was as startled as I was and asked me to remove the sim card and the battery for he was still in iron chains. Before I could see where he put them, my attention was stolen by a voice that came from the other room. "Hi, hello. Who are you? How many did they bring?" "Three", I replied shortly. He followed up with a question "what's your case?" Again I replied briefly "border crossing". And the speaker behind the wall, whose thin and clear voice led me to think of him as a kid closed the conversation by saying "Oh, don't worry. Everything will be alright".

We were able to talk through a tiny whole prisoners have made in the wall partitioning the two rooms. I wanted to ask them if the prison was a permanent prison or just another the hundreds of "hot-spot prisons" found in Eritrea. Just before I did, the door opened and the guard by the name Tesfai opened it and said "You two, come out!" and he led us into the other room, leaving Rezene alone in the room.

The rooms were 3 by 4 and completely windowless. Their roof was zinc with nothing beneath it though a bit higher for anyone to touch it. The door was also zinc and made 10-cm shorter than the length of the door-opening to let air in, which of course practically didn't work. It was very hot and we all took off our jackets and became bare-chested. Generally the zone is extra hot between April and June. The airless rooms were more like a cooking oven than rooms.

The walls were full of messages left by prisoners, mostly their names and where they were originally from like Asmara. There were so many names that made me think the rooms must have been built long ago. But the wall and the doors seemed pretty new. I had to ask the prisoners who were already in the room. They were three and all in their teen years. I imagined they were caught trying to cross the border too. But the two younger ones were members of Division 57 while the third one was a low level guard of the National Security. It had become more or less a tradition of the Public Army to recruit teenagers who haven't seen their first set of beard or their voice to be thick.

Three of them chewed tobacco but were not smokers. That was such a huge relief given the room was 100% closed for air to leave or come in. They were really social and full of hope. The first revelation that came from them was that there were 27 prisoners in the room and 24 in Rezene's room for almost two weeks and left the day before we arrived.

I looked at the room one more time to confirm its size. There was no way 27 people could fit. Where do they stand? Where do they sleep? And more importantly, what and how do they breath? You see, I was a virgin to the army's handling of its prisoners. I was soon to learn it was very possible as long as the well-being of the prisoners is not a concern. What I was told and starting to see firsthand reminded me of two things. One was what my friend Meda used to say: "Don't say you know the cruelty of the Eritrean government until you enter one of its prisons". And the other one was what an old man said once "You are not their sons or grand-sons. They will torture you and feel nothing". I felt the truth in those statements before I even got into Hashferay, the hell of all the prison hot-spots I stayed in.

Around 2pm, I and Abraham were called at the same time. Outside our rooms, we were tied firmly and told to move to separate rooms: me to the left and Abraham to the right. While I appreciated the fresh air, the sun was too hot and the ground burning my bare feet. I was questioned by an interrogator named Zemuy. He had the most grumpy look and scary eyes ever. His office was very small, with seventy percent of it occupied by a table. He was pretending to be busy at work, denying my presence in his room. Then after around five minutes, he said "sit down" without looking at me. I looked around and there was a 20-liter jerry-can where I was supposed to sit on. Noticeable on his table was the same plastic rod used to flog prisoners in Shambko. It was placed directly against where I was sitting, which meant it was put there intentionally to scare me. I wasn't scared at all. There was nothing new to tell them than I already did. I sent my eyes to the paper he was writing and on its header, I read "Anti-Spy Division 57".

Suddenly, Zemuy looked at me and began talking in cold tone "Now, before I beat the information out of you, tell me the whole truth". I replied, in a normal tone "I was going to Ethiopia". He cut me off and said "I don't care about that. I care about this travel documents. Where did they come from?" That was a critical question because still I wasn't aware how Oche was told about. I did give money to Oche to bring me the travel documents but that's the furthest I knew as far as the travel documents are concerned. While that was the truth, I didn't want to give him up easily and put him where I was. I sacrificed Rezene and told Zemuy to ask Rezene about that. "Don't put yourself in a harm's way. He had said you took it from the hands of Oche. Tell the truth". I didn't know what to make of what Zemuy told me. It sounded too real to be something he made up but at the same time, I had no idea what Rezene told them about Oche or the travel documents. "Ok fine, I took it from

Oche's hand" I replied. "And where did he get them?" "I have no idea", I replied him instantly. Zemuy wrote something on the paper and asked me what I had with me when I was caught. I told him "mobile, 1000nfa and shoes". He told me my shoes didn't arrive and he would call the Shambko people. I smiled as he took me for an idiot and pretended to dial some numbers. "There is no phone line to bring your shoes now. You paid 120 for bus so now you have 880nfa with us" and he dismissed me from his office.

After I returned, Rezene immediately started talking through the tiny partition whole: "Tell them I am not a smuggler but was escaping to Ethiopia with you never to return". "Rezene, these are the things you should have told us in the first place. Now they are concentrating on the travel documents only". After Abraham was back, they took Rezene but returned him back after a while. I expected him to say something but Rezene kept quiet. We all knew they have beaten him and he was absorbing the pain in silence.

At 4PM, they passed in one injera (popular bread like food) with a salt-less lentil for six of us. I wasn't sure if they were not feeding Rezene nor I remembered to ask him after that. We were all really hungry and each one picked up two tiny pieces and the plate was as clean as new in no more than three minutes. Very soon later, they asked us if we wanted to pee. The ground outside was too hot for our bare feet but since we won't be allowed out for any reason after 5, we decided to go ahead.

The pee-area was at the center of the compound. It was a 3x3 hole full of dry feces too. I missed the Shambko one because it was at least big enough for 3 people. Much like the Shambko dump hole, the soldiers were all over us, much closer to the dump hole. I and Abraham couldn't go at it at all been conscience of the very close people standing around us and sitting before us. It was a living proof that things will get from worse to worst as we transfer from prison to prison.

I and Abraham were called out unexpectedly at 5:30. We were firmly tied once again and Abraham went to Zemuy while I went to another interrogator whose name I never got. He was much kinder than Zemuy and greeted me warmly upon arrival. He noticed my arms were aching due to the firm rope tied across them through my back, and got up to loosen the rope a little bit. He started talking by firing the hard truth: "Where were you all those years?! Crossing border is over now. You were late". "I don't know", I replied quietly. "And when you finally decided to flee, you chose Ethiopia. You know, if you had in fact crossed, you would have been forced to talk on their radio all that fabricated non-sense". I didn't reply to that last comment. After that, he just asked me a series of biographical data and took my finger print and signature and dismissed me back to my cell.

Before the sun was gone completely gone, two boys and one girl joined us. The girl was left outside under a tree shade while the two heavy smokers joined our cell, increasing the number of prisoners in the tiny cell to 8 while Rezene remained isolated in his own cell. Our cell began to be heavy and fully airless. To make things worse, one of the boys was heavily addicted to smoking and started smoking. The smoke couldn't find a way out nor was air coming in. Since they were all smokers, the let I and Abraham stay close to the only air-opening of the room at the bottom of the door. It wasn't much helpful for it was a windless night.

At that moment, we heard some disturbance outside and we all put our heads to the room opening. We didn't look at what was happening entirely but we understood the girl was sick and they were trying to help her out. Her friends told us she is not healthy while the members of the division (57) told us there is no medication for prisoners at all. All we were hearing was the girl sobbing and the clueless guards asking what her problem was. At some point, she stopped crying and eventually went to sleep, probably out of exhaustion. The men with us told us they came from Asmara and were caught on suspicion of attempting to escape Eritrea, to Sudan or Ethiopia; a charge they denied. I didn't know their fate for I left them behind soon.

It was time to sleep and we all laid our heads towards the door, in the hope of getting fresh air throughout the heavy evening. The pressure in the room was getting higher but slowed down after around midnight. It is apparently a common happening of hot areas. The room was too small for all of eight of us to lay down in the same direction at the same time so three had to sit at the end of our feet for a few hours then somebody wakes up to give them a sleeping turn. We began to curse and complain. The youngest prisoner raised his voice "Be very thankful guys. We are only eight people here. There were 27 of us until yesterday!" He was right. We indeed need to be thankful. For me and Abraham, we would sleep without our hands tied up and our chest almost glued to the rough ground. That ended up Good Friday, a day Abraham would have spent fasting and going to Church while I would have been at home for the most of the day.

The next day, Me, Abraham and Rezene were called out at 8AM. The guard by the name papa Tesfai (Tesfai is not really old but he was referred as aboy/papa out of respect because he was generous and soft-hearted) began to tie us up one by one as two young soldiers stood by on alert. Aboy Tesfai was repeating "Don't worry, this will all come to pass. Be strong". Half way, one of the young soldiers said "Aboy Tesfai, let them wash their faces first. I will fetch them water". It was a very beautiful and kind gesture. Papa Tesfai agreed and we drunk cold water and washed our faces. To this day, I remember the way the soldiers were looking at us. It was full of pity and compassion. If there was a way, I am sure they would have slipped us out to freedom. Papa Tesfai returned to tying us up, which wasn't something he wanted to do but had no option. Since we were going to be on the road, we must be tied firmer. As we were led towards the exit, the younger soldier behind us said "Don't worry. You get jailed, you get freed. It happens sooner than you think". I turned to look at him and smiled and said: 'Thanks habibi'. The merciless thugs who forced such innocent and loving kid into a soldier were not only arrogant idiots but brainless.

We were sure we would go to Hashferay but we saw no lorry, the usual means of transferring prisoners. But then we stopped around a clean, white, two wheel drive Toyota pickup. Papa Tesfai looked at three of us and disappeared after saying "Be strong." It was obvious he didn't want to stay any longer and see our transfer into yet another prison. We figured why they were taking us with a Toyota vehicle. Easter was the next day and having border-escaping prisoners around during the holiday could take the fun out of it as they have to be on constant watch and alert, especially for smugglers like Rezene. It was why there was no intensive questioning and everything was done in a hurry. Otherwise, it was extremely common and typically expected to enclose people in extreme conditions. After I have arrived to Hashferay, I was still in wonder how 40-50 prisoners came from the two rooms in Barentu? I considered myself somewhat lucky to have stayed with only seven people for one night in the Barentu prison.

Zemuy and one other soldier in civil clothing and their driver where on front cabin. The three of us were on the back cabin while a soldier with a gun was in standing on alert at the back. The car joined the asphalt road but took the turn towards Tessenai instead of Keren, as we expected. Rezene turned to me and whispered "It is not going to Hashferay. They are taking us to Aderser". At that time, I didn't know where Aderser prison was located but imagined it must be in Tessenai. From the tone of his voice, I felt as though Rezene knew Aderser and hates it.

Once again, the driver skipped the path towards Aderser and continued towards Tessenai. We reached the most famous and strictly controlled Tessenai security check point and the car took turn to the right and stopped. Security guards came and checked the travel documents of Zemuy and his collogues. Even though it was obvious we were prisoners with our hands tied with ropes and chains and looking exhausted, pale and plain tired, the guard asked who we were. "They are prisoners from Barentu", Zemuy replied and the car was allowed to pass.

The prison we arrived is typically known as "Under Tessenai". The word under is used exactly as English, in reference to the underground cells and torture centers found there. It is not a permanent prison nor fully equipped. Instead, it is a torture center where prisoners are kept until they believe what they are accused or suspected of.

As we got off the car, we were surrounded by guards of Under Tessenai with their guns in place. We were told to sit on the hot ground burning our feet and the hot son hitting our heads. Zemuy went into the nearby small office with our national ID cards, the fake travel documents, mobile phone and money.

One of the guards started engaging us in a conversation. It was a surprise for me since all that I have heard about Under Tessenai is cruelty and inhumanity that interaction from soldiers at softer level was unexpected. He looked at me and said "Were you escaping?" I nodded. "Was he leading you?" he continued looking at Rezene. It was none of his business for he was just a guard but I know I must be polite for I will be under his control for as long as I remain there. Again, I nodded. Rezene interfered right away without been asked "We were both escaping. No leader." The guard smirked and said "Man, we have seen a lot here. Don't put yourself through hell". Rezene smiled back, "You are right brother. But it is the truth".

Zemuy got out and someone called "Rezene" from the office. Rezene stood up and found his nightmare; the mobile phone I have seen in Barentu fall from somewhere in his body. The soldiers were shocked and the Tessenai guards blamed the Barentu guards for not thoroughly searching us. The guards of Barentu prison were silent, with their eyes wide open in surprise and horror. Rezene was thoroughly searched and they took away his watch, which is the only material we are allowed to keep. As for me, the youngest guard by the name of Ibrahim told me to stand up and tried to intimidate me. "Give up anything you have hidden voluntarily. If I find them myself, I will mix you up with the ground". I wasn't scared at all. "I have nothing. Search me". He found nothing.

I was glad of my confidence that moment. Because I had five $20bills carefully stitched at the back of my jacket. That money was never caught and it made it back to a trusted friend through a trusted guard in Hashferay.

I was then called to the office. The officer was a short and rather muscular in civilian clothing known as Wedi Keren. He looked at my national ID and started talking: "I know this ID. It was with me in this very office before". "You are wrong", I replied shortly. "I am never wrong. This exact ID was with me" he continued in a harder tone. "No, you are wrong" I stressed out. At that stage, I was familiar with the eyes they give and the tone they use so his attempt to intimidate me failed. Wedi Keren started rumbling about Eritrea and the martyrs. I was fully quite, knowing anything I say could open up a conversation and also, the stuff he was talking about was extra boring and something I heard all my life from the radio in an attempt to brainwash citizens. Either he was done or realized I wasn't buying any of the crap he was talking about, Wedi Keren stopped and began writing my name on the list of prisoners.

After three of us were done with Wedi Keren, we were led to the main spot of prisoners. The area of prisoners was a little smaller than a basketball rectangle. It was completely surrounded by thorns. The North and West sides are full of mountains made up of burned stones while on the east is a plain, clear and empty land. There were three security guards on each side, watching our every move every second of the day. I got to admit: their skill in picking up prisons is really excellent. At first glance, it seems easy to escape from there. But a closer analysis of the area confirmed it is actually hard to run away from a place that is practically open-air. In fact, in all the years it existed, there were only two escapees. The first one was by three men who jumped the fences and disappear into the mountains under the cover of darkness. Everyone was convinced they were tipped and supported by the guards active that night because they literary passed through their fences. The second was by girls. Before their escape, girls were allowed the pee without been accompanied by the guards, who are all male. Their time was limited and they weren't allowed to go close to the mountain found after the empty land. The guards didn't expect girls to be brave enough and escape and so, paid no attention to them until they return on their own for return-count. A few brave girls exploited that mistake and disappeared to the nearest mountain and were never caught. After that incident, the guards go before the girls, stay at a safe distance so they can't see the girls or make them feel unsafe and uncomfortable while still controlling them tightly.

At the center of the field was a shade where many prisoners were asleep or sitting own. To the left were two openings to what I easily knew were underground cells. The prisoners left some empty space for us and brought us water to drink and wash our face. They were all surprised that we came from Barentu because prisoners from Barentu directly go to Hashferay. We didn't tell much nor did they ask much, knowing we were tired and still not done with questioning.

Once I was left alone, I began to see the prisoners around me. There was an old man, aged around 70, sitting at the corner of the shade moaning with pain. I asked the young boy on my right what happened. "His testicles were beaten up during interrogation". There was a young man, around 25, with a lame left leg. I was told again, they broke it during questioning. And at the back, there was a short, thin man in his mid-forties sitting down on his shoes with his shirt off and feet oiled. He was beaten on the back at the start of his interrogation. Then they moved on to beating him in the sole of his feet after he refused to believe in the accusation. After a while, he was no more able to endure the torture and agreed to all their accusations. The man, who came to Hashferay with me, was unable to walk and suffered from severe pain if anything touched his back.

And there was a mentally disabled youth from the Gash Barka region. He was in an overly dirty gown, typically worn by Muslims but extremely common in all settlers of Gash Barka region regardless of faith. That boy touched me more than all others because he couldn't fit in with us. He would spend his days sitting down directly under the cruel sun. And worst of all, he would search the ground for tobacco others have chewed and spitted out and chew it afterwards. He knew nothing except his name and would reply to a call of a name he shared with a couple of other prisoners. His mental disability didn't set him free.

I remember one day, three prisoners washed his body and his cloth by force and it was the first and the last time I saw him smiling.

Those four prisoners were more than enough to give me shivers. I stopped asking what had happened. There were close to thirty prisoners in the small space, with many showing obvious signs of pain. Almost everyone was caught in relation to escaping the country.

After resting until 2PM, I took the time to socialize and be engaged with the prisoners around me. They told me first about an interrogator known by "John Cena". He got his nickname after the wrestler John Cena for he barely asks prisoners any question and goes straight to hard and unbearable punches with his fist, feet and other materials. I was never able to get his real name but I was told he was from Adi Keyih town, though that is unconfirmed. Because of the countless physical abuse he committed, he is very careful on his every move and barely is seen walking alone or socializing. He left to his home on the morning I arrived so I didn't see him face to face. Based upon what I was told, I considered myself lucky. Because even though my case was pretty clear, he would still have jumped into torture for the hell of doing it. Everyone who went through his questioning session told me he puts a whip and other beating materials on the table and is never reluctant to using them should his hands and feet fail to get the information he wanted.

The goal is: at all costs, make the prisoner accept all accusations. And that was the first thing I fully understood. Examination was never based upon cross-questioning or intelligence but the use of torture and intimidation. It is not the truth they are after but what they want to hear and a confirmation of their suspicion, even if it is completely out of line. What made it so different from the beatings of Shambko and Barentu is that Tessenai investigators are open about it. They are not afraid to hide their identity. Everyone who got tortured knows the name and face of the person who tortured him. The reason is that they have done it for so long that it has become part of who they are. They know there is no way out now. It is not something that can be covered anymore. The best they can do is not to be seen or found alone because given the chance, anyone who been through their torture wouldn't hesitate to kill them.

The beatings start in a wild fashion at first. It is all a bunch of fists and kicks falling randomly on the prisoner. That is then followed in a more orderly fashion using plastic and rod whips on the back and ass. Then it develops into a more or less scientific torture. It is something they got from years of experience and at the heart of it is denying the prisoner any kind of mobility. They have mastered the art of torture that the very simple chairs they use to sit down on typical day becomes an excellent torture materials when they are required to do so. They turn the prisoner to any position they want and beat the hell out of him. One of the most famous areas of beating is the sole of the feet. It is very painful with the possibility of making the prisoner disabled and sterile permanently. There were many cases in which prisoners who been through so much torture were forced to be on a wheelchair or use walking sticks for the rest of their life, not to mention childless. Muscular joins like ankles, knee-cups and elbows were popular choice for they inflict sharp and long-lasting pains. They speak extremely few words during torture, with the word "believe" been the most common one. The beating stops the very minute a prisoner says "I believe", which makes him responsible for crimes he may not even have committed, at all or entirely. Not been able to endure all the pain, many prisoners believe in big crimes that lead them to prison for years.

Unsurprisingly, many prisoners are left unable to walk back or are left unconscious. It is so casual and typical view for the beaters and the prisoners. The beaters would just leave the room, telling one of their guards to call prisoners and carry their fellow prisoner and bring him for further beating the next day. At times they give us cooking oil so that we can massage the very people they tortured while they are sure it will continue tomorrow.

Let me tell you one of the tortures I witnessed firsthand during my stay in Under Tessenai. One time, they were questioning a guy named Yosief from the town of Barentu. They suspected he was linked with smugglers but he resisted their beatings and denied all their allegations. As each day went by, the beatings became harder and harder to the point his back skin began to wither off. On the eighth day, Yosief was seated on a chair facing backwards so his chest rested on the chair and his back exposed to John Cena. His hands and legs were pulled out then tied together so he won't move. Then John Cena started beating and beating his back. "Tell the truth!" John Cena screamed and screamed. "You want me to admit something I never did!" Yosief insisted. At some point Yosief's body became numb, followed by a state of unconsciousness. After two hours, John Cena noticed Yosief wasn't making a single noise nor he was moving. So he stopped his beating and asked "Hey, Yosief...are you alive?" Yoseif who had a mental problem caused by bullet which busted in into his head during the Ethio-Eri war, didn't respond. John Cena opened the door to let air in and then called prisoners to take Yosief and massage him with cooking oil. Of course, the beating continued the next day and I left him there in Under Tessenai undergoing daily beatings every afternoon. John Cena was tired of beating Yosief and stopped the beating after nearly three weeks. But Yosief was jailed for seven months because John Cena believed he have something to do with smuggling even though Yosief didn't accept the allegations nor John Cena had any evidence. Many had passed through an even longer and harder torture than Yosief. While everything about it is sad, it hurts to know there is no one to be held responsible or even be questioned.

Under Tessenai welcomes at least three new prisoners each day in week days while six or more on weekends. The prisoners come from all bordering towns and from within Sudan. The investigators of Under Tessenai were emotionless perhaps because they see so many new prisoners each day and the beating becomes a routine, essentially killing any mercy and love any human can possibly have.

When new prisoners arrive, they immediately begin to imagine what they will face and the physical brutality they will endure. Some do agree with themselves to believe in anything they are told to believe and avoid the beating. The psychological effect of seeing other prisoners in pain and disability is quite high. I wasn't personally worried because there was nothing new to tell them in my case. The other prisoners replied "They never have enough. They will look for more somehow. Just be ready to face it all". It didn't change what I was thinking but primarily because I was obsessed with what Rezene will go through. I was sure, without ever asking him, that he won't admit to their accusations. He won't have more than two questions to talk before the beating starts. Rezene, whose spirit was still strong and high, rebuked the other prisoners: "Why do you scare new comers like that?! The investigators are men like us." And I can feel he meant it. There was some truth in it too. A prisoner can fight and resist their torture, like Yosief did and get a significantly low prison time. If Yosief had accepted their charges for failing to endure the torture, he would have been in prison for no less than 2 years with half of that time been in shoe.

At one point, two high school teachers named Ema and Mengis were caught in Forto Sawa, a town close to Sudan. Of course, they intended to go to Sudan but they endured all the physical torture and survived a month in shoe in Aderser prison. They were sent to Hashferay and were jailed for seven months because the investigators were convinced they were indeed escaping to Sudan but refused to believe in it and no evidence could be found. And that unproven suspicion caused a month long torture and seven months of imprisonment.

Saturday was quite relaxed for us, considering how we were living since

Wednesday. We weren't chained and there was enough fresh air to breath. There was protection from the Sun somehow and enough water to drink and take bath. The days go by with us chatting about our capture, what's to come and general living. I noticed there was no lunch as lunch time had passed without anything. The three of us were particularly hungry since we haven't eaten anything since the day before. I and Abraham had 30nfa but there was nothing to buy in the isolated compound.

At 4pm, the guards began saying "Pee time! Pee time!" The ground was still quite hot but I decided to go for we haven't done in waste since we were caught. Around 10 prisoners were lined up to be counted. Then two soldiers go before us and we follow them after around 20minutes with two soldiers on our side and two at the back. Except one soldier, all the rest had their guns. The waste area is to the left of the compound, a 10 minute walk. It is in a plain land and in a wider space. There was always an empty spot to step a feet in. The space between sitting and standing prisoners wasn't that bad, unless you hate seeing someone defecating or you hate been seeing doing it. The time allocated was around seven minutes, which is typically long in Eritrea's prison hours. The spot and the space are always the same, even if there are 50 prisoners coming out. The reason the number of prisoners was few that afternoon was because of the burning ground and its tiny thorns. After each step, one would stop walking to take out a thorn from the bed of his bare feet. Because of that, many prisoners prefer to escape the afternoon pee time and keep it quiet for the night.

Preparation for dinner starts at 4:30. I found Under Tessenai to be a lot more relaxed and comfortable than Shambko or Barentu but the hunger is unbearable. There is never enough food. The number of prisoners' increases everyday but the food supply never increases. That's because it is designated to be a "Temporary Prison" and so there is no food allocated for prisoners officially. Instead, we are given a little piece of everything from what is allocated to the soldiers. They give us sorghum flour and lentil. We cook everything and share it with the girls who live in hats after the fence. One bread in the style of chapatti, around 30cm in diameter and half a centimeter thick, serves 6 people. If there are more prisoners, they would be distributed evenly to the existing groups. It was why towards the end, more than 10 of prisoners were feeding on one bread.

Since the food was very little, eating dinner and breakfast never take more than five minute. We sit in circle of even numbers, usually between 6-8 prisoners and the food is placed in three or five liter oil jerry-can cut in half to make room for eating hands. Someone who can't eat hot food or is picky about how people eat shouldn't bother to sit down. That cycle continues and gets harder and harder as more prisoners arrive.

At some point, the number of females reached 45 while we reached 40. The hunger was on its maximum. The women complained to our house-leader Elias: "Do you have any brain at all? Six bread for 40 women?! We have kids, mothers and pregnant women here! Please have some sense!" She was right. There were three kids, with the oldest been around 5 years old. There was at least one pregnant girl too. Elias had no any other option except to reduce two breads from ours and give it to them. Still it wasn't enough but the women also understood it wasn't under Elias's control at all. Elias had a talk with the soldier who looks after item distribution to prisoners and was told he can't increase anything at all and we should suck it up somehow. A few days before I left Under Tessenai, the real store manager had come back from his monthly break and told Elias "You are taking higher than usual in fact. It will be subtracted." Elias had to beg him to keep it at the current rate.

Sleeping is still outside, in the open air. It was nice to look at the stars and sleep breathing fresh air. Some soldiers liked to sleep in the underground rooms but most slept in the open air. The guards are active the whole night from their posts.

May 5 was Easter and we were discussing on what to do for the holiday.

We didn't have money. The ones who had money were smokers and tobacco users. The thing is the prison, of all its negligence and carelessness, recognizes the power of cigarette and tobacco addiction and gives back a substantial amount of money found with the prisoners who smoke and chew tobacco. In a desperate attempt to get some money, I have told the registrar who registered my money and mobile but he looked at my teeth and lips and said "Shut up! I know who smokes and who doesn't!" The smokers know they will not have a chance to get more money and so they are very reluctant to share their money, which is understandable.

While the talk was going, I and Abraham were called at the same time. We walked a few meters from our gate and then I was told to continue walking alone while Abraham waits sitting down under a leafless tree. I walked straight to a small room on the left. It was hard to imagine the head of the investigators and one of the most influential men of Command 1 Tesfaldet conducts his questioning in such a room. It seemed newly built, with the bricks fully visible and was isolated from all the other housings around the area.

It was even more depressing and dull inside. The small window looking to the main office was closed and Tesfaldet was on his desk with a notebook and an A4 paper. If they intended to make the room as depressing as possible, they did one hell of a job. At that moment, I tried to imagine how much more depressing and cold the underground torture cells must be.

It was the first time I saw the famous Tesfaldet. He was bald and muscular. As pretty much all investigators, he had a frown face and cold appearance. He signaled me to sit down and I took the chance to explore the room with my eyes. There were no beating materials in sight at all. It was odd since the past two investigators I saw had their torture equipment's right on the table for the world to see. I thought it might be under his table. But the case was different. Tesfaldet actually likes to ask questions first before he began beating prisoners. He does employ the technique of cross-examination and follow up questions to some extent. Should he not be satisfied, he surprises prisoners with his excellent use of his hands. Not only he is muscular enough to cause some serious injury and pain, he knows where it hurts and how it hurts the most. Should that fail, he transfers his victims to shoe specially named after him: "Tesfaldet Shoe". The shoe is found across the asphalt road and contains a series of underground cells that are big enough to hold only three people. For extreme cases, there were cells meant for only one person with no room for sitting down. In fact, many had their arms tied to the ceiling so they won't sit down for days. I have never, personally, heard of anyone who came out of those cells without accepting all accusations. As the guard told us when we first arrived, prisoners come out in the worst physical shape and pain when they finally come out.

Tesfaldet woke me up from what I was wondering by speaking in unexpectedly soft and gentle tone. "Ok. There was no reason for you to come to Tessenai from Barentu. You should have gone to Barentu and to Hashferay then to your home. But you are here because there is something unclear about your case." He asked me all the questions I was asked before and within five minutes, I signed on the A4 paper and left his office. Abraham entered while I joined the other prisoners. Rezene was very quick to ask "Who was he? What did he ask you? He returned you quickly." "It was Tesfaldet and he asked nothing new at all." I replied in reassuring voice.

Abraham was there for no less than 15 minutes. Rezene was more bothered than I was and turned back to me "I am worried. He is late in there". "No, no...don't worry. It is going to be ok", I replied trying to lift his hopes up. Before Abraham returned, the prisoners asked for 5nacfa each so we can prepare coffee and biscuits for Easter. Pretty much all of us did. In no more than five minutes, Abraham was back and Rezene was called and returned in no more than five minutes. He told me they had a brief, rather heated conversation with Tesfaldet and that he said to him, word for word "You are a man like me. I am not scared of you."

Tesfaldet replied "Really? Let's meet later on then". As much as I envied Rezene's braveness, I wasn't sure if it was a smart way to dealing with monsters in full control of his future.

At 1:30, some guards were going to Tessenai and we gave them the money to buy us coffee and biscuits. Everyone was looking forward to the ceremony because it was the most we can do for one of the most loved holidays. Rezene told me twice how he looked forward to having coffee after days. Sadly, he was called back for questioning at 3:30pm and I never saw him for the next two months when he came to Hashferay. He was in the shoe underground cells of Hashferay, where he sees the day light for no more than 20 minutes per day to pee. I used to see him pass by and he was still looking high spirited though he was thinner. Though there were obvious flaws in their plans, I felt bad for him. I was sure he will be in prison for no less than three years in a completely isolated prison named Aderser. Prisoners who came with him from Tessenai told me that he was tortured until "the seventh layer of his skin was seen". I have heard unconfirmed rumors about his past; how he was an excellent smuggler and how he was one of the most wanted ones. I failed to see excellence and smartness in his smuggling operation with me to feel the truth in the first rumor I heard. As for been most wanted, Command 1 knows the most wanted ones by heart and I doubt Rezene would have traveled during day light in their territory. I still don't know the list of accusations he admitted nor have any idea what kept him in Tesfaldet's shoe cells for two months. I imagine they were interested in his past, particularly how many times he had smuggled people to Ethiopia, how he knew the safe route (in other words, who tips him) and what he did with his money. A few days after his arrival, he asked me for shorts and T-shirt and I gave him the only spare I had with permission from the guards who carefully accompany them every step of the way. Rezene left to Aderser prison in July 2013 and that was the very last time I saw or heard of him.

Returning to Under Tessenai prison, the number of prisoners reached 120. It was too much for the little compound. The sleeping space was getting smaller, not to mention the hunger we were going through. The worst of all was however the fact that no decision is made in the prison. We all had to go to Hashferay prison for anything to happen to our cases. There were rumors that prisoners are forgiven on Independence Day (May 24). Some of the prisoners were members of the armed forces which meant they are supposed to be jailed in prisons of their respective army units. And those prisoners who have not yet been through the army head to military training camps. It was why we were all in a hurry to leave to Hashferay and see what happens.

The guards of Under Tessenai prison weren't particularly mean and hostile. That level of softness towards prisoners didn't come naturally though. They know if they ever make it to the nearby towns such as Tessenai, their life is in danger of been taken away by former prisoners or anyone who have heard of them. There was one soldier named Efrem. He was always loud, talkative, and bossy and never walks without a rod in his hand. During my two weeks in Under Tessenai prison, I have never seen him hit anyone with the rod. The best he did was screaming. When I came to Hashferay, I was told he is from the town of Tessenai and one Sunday, he went there for a wedding and some youngsters beat him and left him thinking he was dead. He was in the hospital for nearly two months and came out with important lesson: to never put his hands on any prisoner. Ibrahim, the guard who searched me when I arrived, was the most feared and mean soldier at that time. He was the youngest, barely seventeen years old and already head of what is called a "row" in army language. He got worse once they gave him this rank. Lucky for us, Ibrahim was sick from the third day of my arrival until the day before I left. One thing prisoners from Tessenai used to repeat time and again was "We will cut his throat". As much as I hate the idea of a human life been taken away like this, I did feel their anger. At times it requires a human life to save the life of others.

Sometimes, they used to force us plough the weeds in a nearby farm land they were preparing for the rainy season. It wasn't something anyone enjoyed because the land was full of thorns that really penetrate our feet and the sun was merciless. Some of the days they were kind enough to let us take shoes from the huge collection of shoes they take away from prisoners. And some prisoners used to be taken away to Tessenai, at the head office and residence of Tekle Manjus (blind Tekle as we usually call him is Brig. General and commander of Command 1). The job there was a packaging plant seeds for sell and distribution. The house was also where tyrant president Issais stays whenever he visits Tessenai.

It was at this time three boys and one girl, all aged 15 from the southern town of Adi Keyih and four soldiers joined us. The sleeping space became visibly narrow and the soldiers themselves hated the high number of prisoners, especially since we were consuming food ingredients allocated for them and the higher the number, the more on-guard they need to be.

On Thursday, May 16 one soldier came with our ID cards and a document. He called our names and we knew we would go the next day. We were all excited to leave the hunger-filled Under Tessenai for something we hoped, based upon what he heard then, was better. As expected, the next morning at 8:30, a Scania brand blue lorry came and we were called one by one towards it. There were 43 men and 44 women. First, the women were loaded to the front side of the lorry. Then smugglers were taken in pair and handcuffed with each other. After they are loaded, the muscular and bigger prisoners were handcuffed with the remaining handcuffs. The remaining prisoners were made to put their hands to their backs and tied with a strong rope.

I and another prisoner were the last one to be boarded as we had to move near the office to bring two sacks of charcoal. Charcoal and wood is not allowed for transportation and prisoner vehicles are excellent ways to making the transfer from town to town since they can't be stopped for checkup at security and contraband check points. We put it at the end of the truck and stood up waiting for the guards to tie us.

Ibrahim, the guard dimmed the cruelest of all at that time, came to me and tied me up really loose and softly. I sat on top of the charcoal, while the majority of the prisoners were on the hot iron floor of the truck and so cramped with each other, all facing towards me. For some reason, Ibrahim showed me a great love that time and even brought me a three liter oil jar which we used to eat food in and store water in later on. Despite his dark history in the lives of prisoners, Ibrahim had shown me great kindness to which am grateful. Except me and the other guy who helped me carry the charcoal, everyone was seated in a constant fashion: one person sits down with his legs open. Then another person enters that space and opens his legs too, making room for another prison. That way the lorry that can't hold more than 50 people normally is able to hold more than 80 prisoners.

Six soldiers, with three having guns and the other three with rods were on the edges of the truck. After confirming everyone was tied and well positioned, the truck left the compound at 9:15AM and I left Under Tessenai prison behind me.

There was no much new thing on the way. The sun was getting warmer and warmer. It was particularly visible on the other prisoners for they were feeling the heat of the engines and the hot iron under them and the powerful heat of the sun above them. I had only the sun to complain about, considering my comfortable seat on the charcoal. It was at this time I noticed something unexpected from the girls on the bus. Most of them were young and seemed to be on a joy ride. They were flirting with the soldiers, exchanging phone numbers and talking of future meetings. That part was fine for it distracted the soldiers away from constantly telling us to look down and keep quite. What shocked me was when they started stretching their head kerchief's for the guards. I really couldn't figure that out because the guards will be back with the truck so what's the point of showing them such favors when there were poor prisoners under them, tied, cramped and burning from the bottom and above? The only two women, in their 30-40s, shared their kerchiefs with the prisoners in front of them, which created a pleasant view for me as they were in front of me.

I wasn't familiar with the nature of women before that. Upon arrival to Hashferay, I whispered to my friend Samson from Keren about it and he quoted a famous saying in our culture: 'Expansion of a girl's hips doesn't mean her mind is growing'. I admit that I found it unbelievably sexist and been pro-women in many topics, I did understand why our forefathers had to say it based upon what I just saw on the trip.

We reached the outskirts of Barentu and we were told to dive our head down. That is done in order not to be seen by residents. Everyone knows the truck is transferring prisoners but it was one of the safety measures they apply during any mass-transfer of prisoners. If anyone, by mistake or not, raises his head up, any of the guards is entitled to drop their stick or the butt of their gun on his head. It is common for a few prisoners to bleed in their head on such journeys because of such actions.

We got out of Barentu quietly, thanks to the Sun which took the energy out of the talkative young girls and the soldiers. We drove for around two kilometers in what can be called absolute silence. Then everyone was awake with a scream and call of their Gods and other names when the truck came to a hard stop by crushing to a big hill on the left side. No one had any idea except the car tried to move backwards one time and the driver stepped back in and stopped the engine. The soldier sitting on the edge behind me dropped his gun on me and my friend Aman who was sitting on my right. Amid the wails and cries, the soldier on the front climbed and started shouting: "No body move! No body move!" One girl was crying "Oh God, oh God!" and he turned his attention to her: "You bitch! Shut up!" And the soldiers immediately jumped down to the road and surrounded the car.

The problem was the driver realized the brakes weren't working. He drove without brakes for the first 1Km after we left Barentu. He was looking for the perfect spot to turn the truck 90 degrees and crush it to a hill and bring it to a sharp stop. If he hadn't done so, the path after the crush point was steep zigzag that could have surely claimed the life of everyone on the truck. I admired his expertise for he selected a perfect spot: the hill had water running paths on its leg with concrete ends, which tackled the front set of tires of the lorry as it tried to move back words on impact. He and the soldier with him jumped out of the lorry right after impact so that they wouldn't be wounded by the soon-to-be crushed front glass. It was definitely a quick and great decision.

After thirty minutes, Police traffic came from Barentu and thanked the driver enormously. I heard him say "You are a hero!" Some prisoners pointed at the young children, aged 4 and younger on the lorry with us and said "It is their innocence that saved us today". One way or the other, we were all grateful and blessed to have survived the kind of accident that had claimed many lives of Eritrean prisoners or soldiers. As it so happens, the health of vehicles isn't put to taste prior to transferring soldiers, let alone prisoners.

From that moment on, it was a long time waiting for a replacement lorry. The guards were bored and started losing watch. They let all the girls and the 12 year old boy to come down from the lorry and entertain them. Those of us with a rope tying our arms loosen them up step by step, to the point it was symbolic. The ones who had iron handcuffs didn't have that option but were sat down comfortably. The young girls were flirting with every car that passed though that meant getting us bottles of water.

As the prisoner sitting comfortably overlooking all the rest prisoners, I was wondering who will try to escape. When I think about it now, I don't think there was a time in the history of Eritrea's endless prisoners who got a chance to escape as we did. It was common for prisoners to try escape from a moving truck. Not only was our truck stopped but the guards were completely lost in the fun and flirtiest girls. I hated the girls at that time but looking back, I wonder if they were acting on purpose, to give us the chance to stage an escape attempt? The truck was facing a hill that could be climbed and is easy to walk up. The other side was completely steep cliff that if one was to see his chances of rolling down there, no bullet can get him though the stones there but collide with the stones is a fair expectation.

But then who wouldn't consider that as a better opportunity? All eyes were on the smugglers obviously. Even the expected Independence Day mercy won't have an effect on them. They know they will be stuck in prison for the next 2-4 years. It is quite hypocrite of me to expect them to take the first dangerous step when I was in a better state to do it myself. May be they were waiting for someone to break the ice too? Based on history, if the lorry was full of smugglers to Ethiopia, there would have been an escape attempt for sure. That is an almost common occurrence from a moving truck, let alone a still truck.

At 12:30, Tesfaldet was called and stopped for few minutes and made his way towards Keren. At 2PM, a Sino-truck came up and stopped alongside the lorry we were on so we would be transferred to the Sino-truck without touching the ground. It was big truck and we were all forced to sit on its hot floor. The journey from there to Hashferay was very bumpy and fast. We all suffered, including the guards who couldn't sit down still for the truck was jumping up and down.

We knew we reached the town of Hagaz after almost all the girls screamed. Most of them were from the town. The truck turned to the left at the entrance of Hagaz and marked our arrival to Hashferay Detention Center around 4:30pm.

As we come close to the prison itself, we noticed a fairly big square fenced with stones. There were prisoners moving around and a large number of rags and clothes hanging down. At the very center was a shade made of tree trunks, just like the one in Under Tessenai. Given its size, we felt the number of prisoners visible were very few. Had they already been granted the Independence Day mercy? But then, one of the youngest prisoners on board with us, nick-named Slsi, 15, spoke up:

"You can't see it from here. There are big underground halls where the prisoners are right now". Before we could inspect the compound further from the distance, the truck stopped in front of the office, near the compound and we were unchained and left the lorry.

We all raced to sit close to a wall which was throwing a few shadow to the ground. It was a small shadow but it was big enough to protect our head if we stick it to the wall. The Sun in Hashferay felt somewhat different and new. It was almost 5 but it showed no sense of softening down. Not more than five minutes later, a man with big belly and in civilian clothing came out of the office with paper and started screaming: "Get of the shadow and stand in line in the Sun! You don't deserve to be in the shadow!" and we all moved right to the center of the shadow less spot, where the ground was hotter than the Sun itself. He started calling our names to confirm he is accepting the exact prisoners sent from Under Tessenai. After that, those of us with mobile phones were separated. We went into another office one after the other. The soldier there was named Mulgeta, from the town of Mendefera. The table was full of caught mobile phones. Mulgeta wasn't rude nor he had that much interaction with prisoners but that day, he was extremely rude. Right after I stepped into his office, he asked me if I am a smuggler in harsh tone. I nodded my head no and he asked me its number. Mulgeta opened my Nokia 5230 touch mobile but couldn't close it back. I approach his table to help him but he said "get back!" with so much of arrogance and hatred.

After this procedure is done, they took all the smugglers first alone into the compound. Then we followed them in and a soldier named Saleh (typically called Zebra) counted us in and led us into the compound too. The girls were taken to their hall, which was a brick house built within a small square of stones as a fence.

Right after we entered the main prisoner compound, we were called to pee. Everyone who came with me volunteered while I stayed with all their property. I took the chance to observe the new surroundings.

There were small rooms, as tall us 1.5 meters; prisoners built themselves using sticks and rags. They were connected with one another and they were holding prisoners there away from the sun. To my right was another tree house shadowing two water tanks, from which prisoners get water on specific time of the day. I looked back and saw prisoners appearing and disappearing from nowhere; the underground halls. But the thing that caught my attention the most was the sight of an old man who can't control his balance as he walked and had an eyeglass that was obviously for a tough eye problem. "Why would they prison such an old man at a military facility?" At that minute, a boy, aged 13-14 come and sat down with me. He had shoes and it got me to check the other prisoners. Many of them had shoes; some different for each feet; some very old but they had shoes. I wanted to ask him where I can get one for my feet were burning from the hot ground and the gravels were about to make holes in the soles of my feet. But he started asking me questions about us, where we come from and how many, which led me to ask him how many prisoners were there. "Almost half of the prisoners are at work now and will come back". The only thing I can imagine was the size of the underground halls that host all those prisoners.

After those prisoners came back from work, it was dinner time. We were made to sit down in circle of ten prisoners each and given one basin with 20 breads in it; 2 breads per one prisoner. We cut all our bread into tiny pieces and took it to a prisoner who was giving lentil sauce. One spoon of lentil is served per prisoner so our basin got 10 spoons. We then were given one hot cup of tea for each of us. Since we didn't have cups, we put them in Coke plastic bottles we have brought from Under Tessenai with us and shared it among us.

We ate the food entirely, with nothing left at all. We were hungry. We had been hungry. The food was much more abundant and delicious than anything I ate in the last 16 days. As expected, dinner time was very short and soon the whistle began blowing. The prisoners began forming squared rows in front of the underground halls. Many elders and children and others began gathering up at the center, empty space.

Saleh called the new ones to gather up in circle in one spot. Then he went on to the rest prisoners, starting the one at the far right. He was counting them before they disappear into their respective halls underground. After the majority of the prisoners were put in place, he came to us and separated 12 of us who have been through the army. He sent us to one of the underground cells on the left. The rest were sent to another hall.

The house leader of the hall we were sent to, John accepted us and led us in. We walked a staircase of 7 steps and we were let in. The underground hall is named Tessenai and my God, it was terrifying. It was dark, overloaded and extremely hot. There was no free space to take steps and all the prisoners were in their boxers for the heat was unbearable. Emmanuel, a guy I know from Edaga Hamus, Asmara called me and I made my way towards him and sat down at his feet.

The roof of the hall was roughly 50 centimeters above the ground, the rest 2.5meters was underground. It was hard to guess the length of the hall, given its darkness but there were 5 tiny holes on the roof, in an area as long as 40-50meters. The tiny holes are supposed to let in some air. Truthfully, they were a big help for it was only through them we were getting fresh air though the air we know is abundant and free is inadequate once we were locked up in windowless hall 2.5m deep. Before I asked Emmanuel any question, an order come from the outside, telling the new arrivals to come out. We were led back to the underground hall on the right named Titanic.

Under Titanic welcomed us with a very strong smell of sweat. There were torches inside and I was able to see it was wider and obviously bigger than Under Tessenai (not the prison in Tessenai, but the underground hall Tessenai I just left from). It was led by Kidane Wedi Ele and Osam. The number of prisoners was significantly higher than that of Tessenai. They were mainly young kids and together, we all seemed like beans in boiling in dish. Pretty much everyone was in boxers only. For once in my life, I was among people as skinny as me; with ribs countable and our stomach stuck with our backs. I found a small spot in the middle of the path and sat down. I took off my t-shirt and started waving it around my chest, in an attempt to cool myself. It wasn't helping and one of the youngest prisoners there told me I was just making it hotter and should stop it.

Much like the majority of people born and raised in Eritrea, I have been through the national military training camp. But it never crossed my mind that's how they handle and treat prisoners whose crime was nothing more than trying to be free and lead a normal life, including the very soldiers who served them and fought all the wars at the order of the very men who built such a prison. My friend Meda was right; you don't know the Eritrean regime until you see its prisons. I was sure the number of prisons had always exceeded the number of schools but I didn't imagine it gets this brutal for their own citizens. It has hard to differentiate the situation from a correctional facility (as they refer to it) from a death-facility.

All this thoughts and complaints started on the very first few hours of my life in Hashferay. Before I could settle my thoughts to anything, Wedi Ele started shouting at the top of his lungs so he can be heard across the noisy hall. "Quite! Quite! New comers, welcome! Of course, you don't welcome anyone to this place but you arrived safely. There are always accidents and tragedies during arrivals so I just meant to say you made it safe. Prison is extremely normal. It's a university. Men and a sack got something in common: they get tied up but are then untied. It is part of life. So be strong and accept the reality." He continued "Now, I will tell you the laws of Under Titanic, which you must follow if we are going to co-exist peacefully.

1. Once we are locked inside, smoking is not allowed.
2. All tobacco must be thrown out on a piece of paper or any other container.

3. We never tell soldiers or guards any conflicts or physical fights that exist in this under; we solve it internally.
4. Talking is not allowed after 7pm.
5. Torch is not allowed except the two I and Osam use to manage all of us.
6. Whistling is strictly forbidden once we are locked up as it is a code of a runaway attempt.

After he confirmed we understood the rules, he went on speaking: "Ya shebab ('Oh you the youth' in Arabic), there is a tradition in every prison which applies to all new comers. All new comers should make a donation for candle. The donation is used to buy batteries for this torch, to buy items for shared holidays, to take care of our sick members. Here, there is no one who has been here for less than a year. Since there is no access to family members or relatives, nothing can come to us. All our pockets are empty so please donate any amount you have." Wedi Ele continued selling the cause to us: "Here, we look after each other. There is no clinic. No one cares about how we live. We got only each other and the donation rotates back to you." Donations started following in from new comers. I only had 10nfa in my pocket and I didn't share it, knowing it is the only cash I and Abraham have for the unknown period of time. After the donations were gathered, Wedi Ele silenced the hall and took the stage once again: "Ok, thank you for your donation. Now it is too hot to give you sleeping spots. It will start to cool down around 10PM and I will tell you where to sleep then. Until then, we do entertainment."

The entertainment was just music but it was really thoughtful. Because when we all talk, the air we breathe gets accumulated and creates a huge pressure because it can't find a way out. At 7pm, there was silence again; it was time for the Islamic prayer of Salat. Some Muslims gathered up on the left side of the hall and started praying while the rest were sitting down or asleep in obsolete silence.

We, the new comers, were extremely tired and exhausted from the long journey and the sun. We wanted to sleep near the spots we were sitting on but there was no space left at all. The prisoners weren't particularly friendly or cooperative either but I soon learned why. You see, as times goes by, one just to feel comfortable for him at any chance he gets. After everything is taken away, the little possibility of comfort and relaxation is to be exploited with some degree of selfishness. And that is not easy to find at all. The sleeping space each one owns is shared and substantially reduced with each new arrival.

After the Muslims prayed, Orthodox Christians started praying and the silence continued. The respect and tolerance of other faiths rituals was very much high and wonderful. After that, the stage was returned to Semir, who continued singing mainly Arabic songs.

At 10PM, Wedi Ele rose up and shouted: "Everyone take your sleeping space! New comers stand in the center section". We all lined upon along the narrow, central path across the hall. And I witnessed people lining up like tuna fish in a can. They left on space between each other and slept in a standard fashion named Cartelo: One prisoner lays down on his right ribs with his head to the wall then the next one with his feet to the wall. That way each prisoner's head is resting on feet of the next prisoner. The hall was divided into five sleeping sections, as illustrated below. Three sections sleep vertically across the hall while the other two sections end at both ends of the hall horizontally. Those two ends are for VIP prisoners and their friends such as Wedi Ele and his friend Semir on one end and Osam on the other end.

I heard the prisoners arguing with each other for shortage of space. Some were trying to cover up any space between them. I was standing at the center of the hall, directly opposite the entrance door. Wedi Ele started giving space on the left section, and it was miserable. He had his belt on his hand and started flogging each prisoner "Leave space! Stick further to your right!" The slaps of his belt falling on someone's body were loud and clear. After they make a little space, Wedi Ele calls one prisoner and puts him in. That is his space.

He reached near me and started beating the hell out of the prisoners. Each fall of the belt on the body was creating the tiny space indeed. He made one for me and I sent my head towards the wall and fell down on my left hand and marked the start of my cartelo sleeping style.

Osam was doing the same thing on the other side. That way the 40 new comers blended in the crowd. That night, the number of prisoners in Under Titanic reached a shocking 264.

The temperature was extra hot and unbearable. We were all shirtless and sweating a lot. Our sweaty skin was rubbing each other and it was the first sign of disgust and discomfort with me, as a new comer. I tried to move backwards but the person on my back was equally sweating.

I started my first night in the prison I saw a lot happening, washing and swimming in sweats of each other and it wasn't the worst night at all.

INTRODUCING HASHFERAY CAMP

Before I talk about the life at Hashferay Camp, let me introduce you the prison itself. It is called Hashferay Rehabilitation Camp officially but I and many other prisoners didn't see the term Rehabilitation in effect so we barely call it that. It is found about 18 km away to the right side of Hagaz, in a mountainous section of the area. Before it became prison, it was famous for been training compound for all ground forces of the nation in their ranger courses. It is why one finds head of bullets in the nearby mountains, especially the ones to the east of the compound. Every soldier who got training there still shivers when he remembers it. The course is not different from any ranger course provided in other places content-wise but the heat and pressure in Hashferay is unbearable. Hagaz is the hottest and dumpiest place in the Anseba region. It is this heat and pressure that forces one to look for a shade at any given time. There are few trees in the area, of which most are thorn bushes that are not friendly at all. The other characteristic of the area is the scarce number of settlers in the surrounding villages, which are very small, with predominantly nomadic settlers.

So when Command 1 selected Hashferay to be their central prison, it wasn't done out of the blue. They surveyed the area for 17 days before they selected the current square for prisoners. Even though it is intended for evil things, I applaud their expertise in selecting the right spot to host and torture prisoners. The compound is at the center of mountains, where guards are stationed at high altitudes. The treeless area added an extra security feature for prisoners don't have a place to hide and guards, should they need to use their guns, have few distractions to aim correctly. It is why escape attempt was extremely rare in Hashferay. True, after we return from work and are enclosed in our square or went into our underground halls, the guards at the highest mountains get back to their stations and only the inside-guards take full charge of us directly. The guards are stationed within the compound itself and outside the compound in all directions of the compound. Other units surround the compound distantly. And finally, the settlers in all the 3-4 villages surrounding the compound are members of the so-called "public army". Though they are fathers or former army members who know the bitter taste of Eritrea's military prisons, they often showed no mercy. The later two react immediately if warning shots are fired from the main guards of Hashferay in times of Prisoner escape attempt.

Prisoners of Hashferay

As the center prison of Command 1, Hashferay accepts prisoners from all prisons of Command 1 as well as the police station of Keren or Anseba Zone. The latter one is particularly odd because prisoners on civilian cases handled by civil police are forced to come to a military prison for no good reason, other than the enormous power Command 1 had one the administration of Keren and Anseba Zone. The other sources of prisoners include:

Asmara: the capital hosts at least two temporary prisons of Command 1. The first one is found around Finland Mission School, hidden in the trees and is underground. While the second one is a villa in a place called Villago and often known as "Da Idirs" in reference to its main operator named Idirs. Prisoners from Asmara come at most twice a month with no more than ten prisoners at once. The prisoners were usually victims of Idirs and his web of snitches. Their story is almost always the same: my friend gave me up.

Anseba Region: The central office of Command 1 is located in Keren and as such, its effect on the region is visible and clear. Command 1 unit in Zoba Anseba is Division 63, which have many small prisons throughout the zone. But the main ones are in the heart of Keren, mainly known as "da Abdu", in reference to the main operator named Abdu and Hagaz.

Gash Barka: Barentu (prison of Division 53) and other small prisons around Barentu.

Other sources were located in Nakfa, Aderser, and Mendefera.

But most of its prisoners come from Under Tessenai, which sends a minimum of 80 prisoners on each trip. It is guaranteed to come twice a month, sometimes more than that. We knew prisoners from Under Tessenai from a distance based upon their number mainly.

On November 1, 2013, eight prisoners arrived through Under Tessenai from South Sudan. It was the time when South Sudan was in chaos and many Eritreans took refuge in Eritrean embassy in Sudan. Those eight have never paid the mandatory 2% foreign-settlers tax and were separated from the rest who paid and brought back to Hashferay for imprisonment.

Hashferay hosts a very diverse type of prisoners. Mothers with infants, pregnant women, old mothers, aged fathers, underage kids (as young as 9 years old), disabled, blind, HIV Positive, soldiers, civilians...you name it. Most youths would lie about their military status and claim to have never been through military training yet. The poorly networked army data and the change of names aids that lie perfectly. That way, a single prisoner can go to the military training camp of Command 1 in Nakfa two or three times. The reason is that the sentence for army-related prisoners is longer and harsher. The administration of Hashferay was very well aware of this incident but they can't do anything about it. During my stay, they were able to remember only one underage boy (15) who was caught trying to escape three times. They recognized him on the third time and put him in shoe with other smugglers after he attempted to fool them. Other than that, they were more than happy to change names and status to the truth instantly should a prisoner approach them. The truth is they never get bored of imprisoning people but they didn't enjoy training prisoners over and over again.

Hashferay prison had crossed its own record of imprisoning all kinds of prisoners on March 25, 2014. On that day, Under Tessenai brought three completely mentally ill people. They were former members of the defense forces who have completely lost their mind in the process. As such, they disturbed the compound completely. However, that wasn't new thing for the guards and administrators of the prison. They have welcomed and sent away many mentally disabled prisoners in a much worse situation.

Typically, members of defense force (other than members of Command 1) are sent to Adi Abeto prison and be dispatched further to their army units where they finish their prison time. Civilians who have never been to the army are sent to the military training of Command 1 (which is unique feature of the Command since all other soldiers are trained in Sawa, the defense central military training site). Members of governmental ministries demobilized from national service or not, are imprisoned in Hashferay for at least 8 months along with all other kind of civilians. That way, the process of new prisoners arriving and leaving continues.

Though it is hard to prove at all, I did hear ones the number of prisoners reaches on average 800 at any given time. Given its small compound, overcrowded underground cells and the never ending transfer of prisoners, one wonders if there is anyone free in the streets of the country at all.

The first thing I noticed in the life of the prisoners was the heavy use of cigarette, tobacco and tattoos. The tattoos were badly shaped and often the same; an eye with tear drops,' I am Sorry mom', 'I love you mom', Cross and bird. But one tattoo did stay out of all of the rest; tattoo of a girl crying sitting down with her head on her knees, covered in her own arms.

Gual-Zara, a girl crying, one of the most famous tattoos in prisoners

The girl had a true history behind it. It is known by "Gual Zara" which means "Girl of Zara". The story is as the following.

Once a girl lost her fiancé/boyfriend and she was going from prison to prison in search of him. She arrived to prison known by Zara and met the administrator. He was known by Wedi Zara. Zara prison, found around Barentu, is known for its extreme cruelty and inhumane treatment of its prisoners. Wedi Zara, one of the most corrupted prison commanders, was in charge and told her that her fiancé is in his prison.

And should she sleep with him, he would find a way to let him go.

She had no option but to obey. Wedi Zara discarded her after he got what he wanted. His last words, as he pushed her out of the compound was 'Get out! I don't want to see you!' Outside, she sat on the dusty ground, put her face on her knees and cried her eyes out. She was insulted, ashamed and betrayed.

That image of her crying was so popular to the point many tattooed her on their arms permanently.

Interrogators have committed such crimes throughout the country at different periods. They find a way to get away with it. Gual Zara wasn't the first nor was she the last victim of the inhumane and manipulative investigators.

Underground Halls of Hashferay

Hashferay is made up four underground halls 2-3 meters deep underground. Their roof is above the ground; at a height of about 50cm. Prisoners would be locked there from 5pm until 6am every day. All of them had 5-6 tiny openings distributed across the roof to let air in. Given the size of the halls and the number of prisoners, those air-holes were practically meaningless especially during the hot seasons. During rainy season, they would be close from the top roof as they let water in, creating an almost airless atmosphere.

To let a little more air snick in, the right side above the ground was built with bricks made up tiny holes. Those holes are so tiny that a bird can't pass through one at all. So, practically speaking, 95% of the hall was underground while the 5% is above ground though it is airless for the most part.

Unintentionally, I have stayed in all the four underground halls at different times of my time there. I consider that a blessing for it gave me the chance to evaluate of them all. Even though they are built in the same fashion, the life style of each under differs based upon its prisoners.

Under Asmara: It is found on the right end of the square, close to under Agordat. It was led by Atie, from Edaga Arbi Asmara and most recognized for its relatively cold temperature inside. That coldness was due to the bigger opening in the right side bricks that let more air in. It is smaller in length but wider. It is probably why it was assigned to prisoners who are members of Command 1. I have slept in Under Asmara for four nights. It was so clean and very orderly in all its forms. They would chat with each other in a calm and low voice that causes no disturbance to the rest. Most of its members are wildly rude on any given day but in the under, they were very polite and easy going. That was thanks to the leadership of Atie. Under Asmara had a relatively constant number of prisoners as Command 1 prisoners finish their prison in Hashferay and few new prisoners arrive to it. In January 2014, around 65 new smugglers arrived when every shoe for smugglers was full. So prisoners in Under Asmara were told to be distributed to all the other under's temporarily when their under became just another shoe for smugglers. My most clear memory of Under Asmara was its neatness except for the rats that move on the sides but were largely ignored.

Under Tessenai: Found next to Under Asmara, it was the smallest of all the under's in both width and length. Its bricks had the smallest holes to let air in as well and therefore, it was without a doubt, the hottest and most pressured under. It was assigned to any prisoner in active service other than members of Command 1. Because its members were part of all units of defense forces and ministries, it was known as "Different Units". It was built to hold maximum 100 prisoners sleeping in cartelo style but more than often, it was stuffed up with more than 140-160 prisoners. Because of its small size, Under Tessenai prisoners had to follow a unique style of sleeping. This is best illustrated in picture, as tried below. Essentially, prisoners on the two sides sleep in a style called

"Bat" because they have to put their leg up the wall to make room for other prisoners and themselves. One can't sleep with full body extension. When we are tired of having our leg up the wall, we would break our knees and put it into the empty space made by the broken knees of the prisoners before us. That way we would create a beautiful view of zigzag with our knees. When there is space, we would sleep on our backs but still with our feet up the wall or to the side as necessary. The people who sleep vertically between the pillars are considered lucky for they can extend their feet length-wise. When there are many prisoners, they would share their tiny space with more prisoners. Those of us who sleep on the sides would have our heads extended across their length, horizontally.

Sleeping Style of under Tessenai

But with all its tiny space, Under Tessenai was hard to leave once one entered it. It had life and some joy in it that makes one never leave it to any other under. The reason is the quality of its members. Most of its members are either relatively educated or experienced with life, which makes the talks quality and mature. It followed different entertainment programs, which included General Knowledge questions, sharing experiences and knowledge, gospel songs and so forth.

Under Titanic: Under Titanic was the very first under me entered. It was also the very first under to be built in Hashferay. It got its name from its length. Under Titanic is mainly for underage civilians who claim to have never been trained in the army and are linked with smuggling people. They are usually sentenced for longer period of time so the number of its papers is mostly constant, in hundreds. Lead by Wedi Ele and Osam,

Under Titanic was poorly managed especially compared to under's Asmara and Tessenai. The immaturity of its members was also one of the causes of its bad management too. Its house leader Wedi Ele was extremely kind at heart, as a leader and person, but he was weak in leadership and management. He had a rather controlling behavior and demands to be the only to be heard and was highly criticized for the bad management of money donated by its members now and then. During the 6 weeks I was in under Titanic, he was the house leader and treasury, which led away to transparency and a lot of dissatisfaction from us. While he was quick to react, Wedi Ele did excel at solving under problems within the under. I recall him reporting a prisoner to the guards once and that time, he was really forced to doing so. He was generally brave towards guards and was highly respected. It was why his request for someone to leave Under Titanic and sleep outside in the open air does get guaranteed easier than anyone else.

Under Titanic had no sophisticated entertainment programs at night. The only type of entertainment was singing, which was overly repetitive but much preferred by the majority. At some point, a couple of prisoners named Semere and Mussie borrowed the General Knowledge tradition of Under Tessenai and applied it. The under wasn't particularly receptive of the change and it never happened again though I and a few more loved the program.

The most significant history in relation to Under Titanic was that it was visited once by Tekle Manjus. He went inside and came out with his fingers blocking the opening of his nasal opening firmly because he wasn't able to tolerate the strong sweat smell Under Titanic was well known for. That smell had haunted the hall for really long time until its members took a bold step of dealing with it in the last couple of months of 2013.

Under Nakfa: Built fully by us, the prisoners, Under Nakfa was positioned to the North and is the biggest of all the halls. It was also one of the coldest halls due its position which favors the wind. In January

2013, Tekle Ewir visited it and said "this hall can hold 300 prisoners". Much like Under Titanic, its members were mostly under age prisoners associated with smuggling. It also hosted many temporarily prisoners so its numbers goes up and down a lot. Led by Mahari, Under Nakfa was tidy. From all the four under's I stayed in, Under Nakfa had the most fights between its members. That was notably visible in its underage prisoners who were in jail for 3-4 years and have lost their temper and patience.

Under Agordat: Found before Under Asmara, Under Agordat is built just like any other under. But it became shoe after number of smugglers and political prisoners increased.

The majority of the prisoners used to live in the Underground halls. Some other prisoners, mostly elders, children and sick people sleep in the open air at night. It also includes ill prisoners, especially diarrhea and malaria sickened prisoners. Those people are believed incapable of living the harsh life of the underground halls. It was a privilege to get out of those underground halls and sleep in the open air. One can see the stars. There is enough space for someone to lie down on his back comfortably. The only drawback is that the nights are not peaceful due to the presence of the guards. In the underground halls, one can wake up in the middle of the night and stand up to pee or move freely from end to end. Outside in the open-air, movement is extremely limited after 6pm.

Standing is not allowed at all costs. When we need to pee into our plastic bottles, we get on our knees and do our business in our bottles. Before it is completely dark, we can crawl to our friends at a short distance. Talking is quite limited and at times, based upon the mood of the eight guards within the compound, the night can be absolutely quite. But we still preferred sleeping outside with all these restrictions and setbacks.

The guards and administration knows sleeping outside a huge deal and privilege. And so, the used to intimidate us by saying (and acting on it) they would return us back to the under's. The most common guards to doing that were Issais Wedi Fichel and Saleh Zebra. Saleh had the most bitter tongue that really find it difficult to utter anything good but I frankly have never seen him return back anyone back to Under practically. Wedi Fichel on the other hand enjoyed returning us to the under's just because he has the power to do so. One time, he ordered the nurse to give him list of prisoners who are medically unfit to sleep in the under's. That evening, he returned 40 prisoners back to their under's. Given the chance, Wedi Fichel would try harder to return everyone back to under. Another guard known for doing similar thing was Ismael. But Ismael does what he does because that's what he thinks his job is while Wedi Fichel was a pure sadist who wants to make the lives of the prisoners as miserable as possible.

It was generally hard to sleep outside. Smugglers and their associates found it hard to leave their under's. Some of us, including me, have found a way to pay some guard a hundred or two and sleep outside.

Shoes of Hashferay

Individuals whose crimes are dimmed high, such smugglers, political prisoners and so forth are placed in seven separate shoes. Their depth is as deep as the under's. Those cells are airless except through the tiny holes of their doors and the small openings of the three bricks on top of the doors. They are designed to hold no more than five prisoners but are often overcrowded.

The dimension of the shoes is about 2 by 4. Yes, picture it. To prisoners can't comfortably sit down facing each other yet due to limited space, they would sit with their legs crossing each other.

The prisoners are easy to recognize by their skin. Due to lack of fresh air, sun and once-a-week bath time, their skin becomes thin and pale, while at times, due to the warmth, it becomes soft orange. They are often weak. As Bereket, a friend who spent a few nights there told me once, they hated coming out to the outside because the sun is too powerful for their skin and weak eyes. In fact, I recall a young man who almost lost his vision after spending more than a year in a shoe.

The shoes are six in number and named Shoe 1, shoe 2 even though prisoners often code-name them such as Sabrina. An exceptional shoe is Agordat, which is much bigger, colder and hosts prisoners who spent more time in the other shoes and got a transfer.

In all the Under's and shoes, there were 700-900 prisoners aged 10 to 90, all genders, religions and all walks of life. And none of us knew our sentence. Until the day comes when our name is called, we don't know for how long we will remain in the prison.

But just like the rest of Eritrea, if you have a powerful man in your life, he or she can get you out with a single phone call without ever stepping feet into the otherwise tough and hard-to-penetrate Hashferay. Let me give you an example. Once, a teenager named Samson, son of a colonel was caught going to Sudan and brought to Hashferay. Don't get me wrong; Samson was very social and required no special treatment at all. He was sleeping; slaving and getting punished just like the rest of us. Within 8 days, his father came and took his home on his private land cruiser. Friends of Samson had to be jailed for as long as 12 months, for the same reason but all because they didn't have a powerful figure to approach the commanders of Command 1. I have absolutely nothing against Samson. He was quite a joy to work with. More than all, it is a great thing to see someone escaping the hell Hashferay.

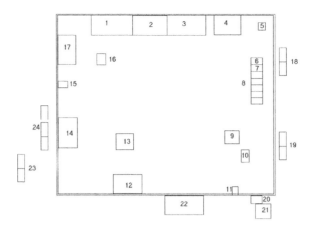

Sketch 1: Main compound for prisoners

Under Titanic

Under Tessenai

Under Asmara

Under/Shoe Agordat

Zinc made bathroom for Col. Tewil

Shoe for diarrhea sick prisoners

Shoe for Col. Tewil

Series of shoe cells

Hat for diarrhea prisoners during the day

Guarding position at night

Door to outside

Internal restroom used by shoe prisoners

Shade mainly for prisoners working in kitchen

The kitchen

Another door to outside

Guarding position at night

Under Nakfa

    18-19. Guarding positions at night time

Shop

Clinic

Women prison

Dorm of Keshi and 1st Group
Guarding position at night

Structure of an Underground hall

<= Above ground part of the halls. Black dots are tiny openings on the frontal part of the cells meant for air transmission ==>

Tiny air-openings on roof of the halls

Underground part of the halls

A wider View of Hashferay

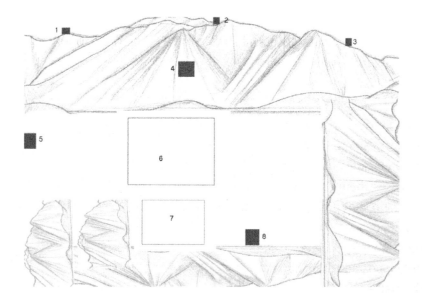

1,2,3 Temporary guards
4 Main guard post (24/7, 365 days)

5 On road guard (24/7, 365 days)

6 Main prisoners' compound

7 Newly built prisoner's compound

8 Main entry gate guard (24/7, 365 days)

OUR DAILY LIFE

Just like any prison, the life of prisoners in Hashferay was very much routine. We wake up at 6am and go to pee for 10 minutes then continue to work in earth dams, buildings, water fetching, wood gathering or any manual work. We come back at 10am to get water for drinking and sit down under the sun until 12 waiting for lunch. And as soon as food is over, a count of all prisoners is done between 12:30 and 1:30. At 2pm, we go back again to work until 4pm then come back to wait for at least an hour for dinner until 5pm then get locked up in our Under's.

All the works were demanding manually and one can only be reminded of slavery. But it wasn't the worst of the daily activities. Everyone hated the mid-day count down because each prisoner has to sit down in the plain field when the sun is at its strongest point. We sit in different groups such as soldiers of Command 1, all other military people, civil and over age men. Usually, the count starts by the elders and ends with us, the different national slaves grouped as "Diverse Units" and so, we had to suffer the most practically. The number of prisoners is held in that group and compared to the number of the previous day. So, if the number of Over Age matches, logic dictates they go to their resting place or under's. Why sit there to fry until everyone is counted? Some of the soldiers do that but often, everyone had to sit down until all the hundreds of prisoners are counted one by one.

It was very inconsiderate because we work the whole morning and go back to work in a matter of minutes.

Those prisoners who don't go to work for any reason had a routine day too. They go to pee at 9am and 3pm and spend the rest of the day on their own activities. There were times we would somehow hide in the under's or so and skip work. But even after the majority of prisoners have left to work, there is no peace inside. The whistle blows every minute, calling for everyone to be out of the under's for possible work. The problem is we are slaves of every unit in Hashferay. And any individual who needs a work force to do some job can come at any time of the day and take as many prisoners as he wants.

It is this boring and routine life that makes the days more miserable. At the end of the day, one gains no experience from the activities.

Food was prepared by prisoners. At that time, the head of the kitchen was Mussie from Liban. He was one of the kindest prisoners I have ever met. He genuinely was concerned about the well-being of prisoners and tried his best, sometimes beyond his limits, to feed each one of us. It was not hard to understand he and his colleagues had to carefully calculate the few amount of ingredients given to them. They were free from the typical day to day labor we had to go through but by all means, their job was much harder than any of our jobs. First, they have to wake up at 3am every day and spend their days in the kitchen for pretty much the whole day. Secondly, it is really hard to cook for hundreds of people with ingredients that never change. The only benefit they had, though I wouldn't really call it benefit, was they can custom cook their food.

Our food was the same every day; one spoon of lentil with two 30gm breads and a cup of tea. More than often, the soup smells like lentil but contains no lentil seed at all. The bread, made from sorghum, is quite dark, salt-less and often very dry because it is baked a day before serving. We are not given plates so we had to get some sort of container or share with others. The most common containers were that of jam jars, cups, tins and anything that can be made to hold something.

Some lucky prisoners used to add pepper and other ingredients to their food. That pepper is smuggled from their family somehow. Those who have money would go further and buy canned fish from the only shop in Hashferay. That number was few at first but as we began bribing and befriending the guards, more and more prisoners were mixing the tasteless food with other ingredients and create edible food. However, the majority had no option but to eat the camp provided food.

Now is good time to thank Mussie. He had gone beyond to make sure we have something to eat, however tasteless and bad. It was better to eat something than nothing at all and he struggled to make sure that happens. One day, the oven was out of order and Keshi, the commander, said in plain words: "just give them bread and quit". Unable to process that order, Mussie went out in search of a fallen tree trunk and brought it back on his shoulders. He and his colleagues had to make fire and be burned from the ground up and the sun above. After lunch, Keshi approached him to say "I knew you would find a way to feed them". While the people we were serving our asses off didn't give a rat's ass, Mussie cared a lot. Mussie was released on bail on March 15, 2014 after five years and three months.

When I arrived to Hashferay, I had 10nfa for me and Abraham and a jacket. The ground of Hashferay was so hot to the point one can't stand steadily for longer than a minute. Many would create shoes out of anything they can find. As long as it stands between feet and the ground, it is considered safe. We would flatten water or soda bottles and make four holes on four corners. Then we insert some thread and tie the threads across our feet. There is no way to throw away shoes just because they are old; they go through multiple surgery or operation with endless threads and ropes. When one finds new shoes somehow, he transfers the old shoes to someone else, which is one of the biggest gifts anyone can give. I suffered for three days and the skin of my sole of my feet began to loosen up. On the fourth day, a guy I have seen in Asmara twice approached me and said "You are friend of my brother Tesfaldet?" I nodded, partly in joy because I haven't yet met someone I know so far. He told me his name is Bereket and he immediately bought slippers and a soap and gave me the remaining 20nfa out of 100nfa. It was such a relief to wear shoes again and to have a soap to wash because we were very dirty with dust and sweat. Aman and Abdu, who come from Under Tessenai with us from Hashferay, gave us 10nfa and we bought slippers for Abraham too.

After months, I found out that Bereket spent the only cash he had in his pocket on me and had to go without a cent in his pocket for long. But it created a wonderful friendship until the day I left. I fixed, stitched and wore the slipper shoes he bought me until my family found a way to send me shoes. Bereket was jailed on January 19, 2013 and to this day (September 2015); he was in jail in relation to the popular immigration case.

My gratitude to Bereket isn't rooted only on the fact that he simply came to my rescue in my worst times but that he gave it all knowing I might never return the favor. Finding a way to get money from family and friends was hard, if not impossible. Many finish their sentences without ever hearing from their loved ones.

The first shoes that made it to me safely from my family.

Some of the works we had to do were near the administrative office. Near there was a shoe storage room and some prisoners exploit a small opportunity they get to steal shoes of any size, kind and sometimes a pair of shoes for the right or left feet only. That was a rather uncommon thing for jobs near the office or the storage area was rare. Sometimes brand new shoes called Shida or Congo would find their way to us for sell. They often circulate by prisoners who have close ties with some guards who bring the shoes from the camp or from other towns for sell. They were at least twice higher than their regular price but get sold out almost instantly. Guards would also buy shoes for us for a bit more cash. In December 2014, my friend Sami brought me brand new Congo shoes and I used them until the day I left and had to leave them at Camp for we were not allowed to wear shoes when transferring to other prisons.

In relation to shoes, I remember one act. Those days, the water distribution truck was in garage and we had to fetch drinking water to all the military units around the camp. Ten of us were selected to fetch water for Division 63 post, which was found behind our camp. The distance between the camp and the source of water was anywhere between 1.5 and 2km. We had to carry a 20 liter jerry-can on our shoulders to the various locations. Among us was a new teenager who hadn't found shoes. We can't walk slowly, whether we have empty or full jerry-can. It was particularly difficult for the ones without shoes. Now, when we reached their post, there were a couple of girls in one of the tents. They were members of Division 63, dressed in full military clothing. We weren't allowed to interact with them but they felt so sorry and one of them threw out her brand new Shida shoe, saying "it is for the boy without shoes". Though that teenager left Hashferay soon to the military training camp and had to leave the shoes behind, the girl had done one of the kindest things any soldier can do. He didn't have the chance to thank her but no doubt he felt over the moon. Generally, members of Division 63 were extremely kind and cooperative. I don't believe they would have punished her even if they had caught her red handed throwing her shoes to him.

Life in the Under's

Life in all the four under's was similar. At 5:30, we stand in front of our under's for the final count of the day. The number of members per under must match the number from the previous night. Once the number is confirmed correct, we are rushed into our halls and locked up from the outside.

I have always been a night man. I would work late night and walk back home in early morning hours. Over the years, I have gotten attached to the sky and its wonderful beauty at night. My friend Samrawit used to miscall me in the middle of the night when there are too many stars or none at all and it was an excitement to go out and see. And that's the one thing I kept on remembering as I went to sleep every night in the under's. There was no sign of star or the moon at all. Some nights are extremely dark that the halls felt like one big cemetery. Of course, with time, I was used even to that. But I figured my love for the night view was just buried shallowly when I was first allowed to sleep outside in the open air after few months. The free night sky view we are all born with seemed different, exciting and the biggest gift on its own. I never slept on my side but on my back and till the last minute my eyes were open.

Back to life in the under's; the first one or two hours are usually noisy as we set upon reserving our sleeping spots, chit-chat and move from end to end. Around seven, the activities slow down eventually and someone takes charge of the hall to start something entertaining. That is very essential to cooling down the halls because when we all talk, our breath creates a much warmer air which doesn't circulate with the outside air because the under's have practically no openings. The calm entertainment contains songs, jokes and narration of stories by a single prisoner. It goes until about 10PM and slowly closes down as we dive into sleeping after a long day of labor.

The sleeping style was the same in pretty much all under's with the exception of Under Tessenai. For the most part, we sleep in cartelo style. Some days are really the worst and we are forced to sleep in an extreme form of cartelo that we usually call mortello. It is cartello but don't allow any kind of gag or air between prisoners.

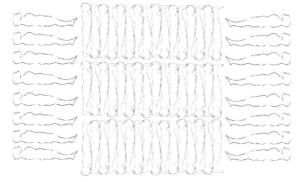

Final sleeping arrangements of under's Titanic, Nakfa and Asmara. The two ends, the comfort zones, are occupied by house leaders and their associates. It is comfort zone because it allows them to sleep on their backs and gives them the space to move around.

Final sleeping arrangement of our under, Under Tessenai

Even though it is not that much, there was some conflict caused due to shortage of space. A few had developed into fights but the conflicts almost never leave the under for the prisoners who fought would be punished severely. Something that was also common is giving extra special treatment to veteran prisoners. That includes giving them the best positions, giving them a little more space so that they can lay down on their back or have a bit space between each other if in cartelo. This was an accepted procedure and one that is common in all prisons. Our under, Under Tessenai, had almost a constant number of 100-120 at any given day so our sleeping style and space was pretty normalized. Since it was small, finding a privileged sleeping space was not easy, even for the house leaders.

Sleeping was not a problem at all. Since we are exhausted by intensive labor works throughout the day, we didn't mind the space or the bed bugs at all. I am sure former prisoners would frown about my understatement of the famous bed-bugs that made our lives miserable. The warmness of the under's, coupled with the soft-wall (where they hide and lay eggs) has made it easy for them to reproduce at high numbers. Due to the hot weather, we sleep in our boxers but with the bed-bug breakout, many prisoners were forced to sleep in their clothing, burning and sweating because it was better than the biting of the bed-bugs. The administration had once heard our cries and complaints and brought some chemicals to spray our under's with but they chemical was already expired and had no effect at all.

And the months between September and December were best remembered in relation to the sleepless nights we had thanks to bugs.

The worst part of life in under is getting sick once the door is locked. Due to the high pressure and heat, some would be knocked down unconscious or be unable to breath. The first thing we do is shuffle something in order to give the ill person some fresh air. Should that not work, the house leader begs the guards outside to open the door and see the ill person. The guards don't like opening the door after it is closed nor were happy to allow one to sleep outside. Sometimes all it took was for the ill person to take fresh air and return back immediately. There were times the ill person gets beaten up if he regains his breath very soon after they he is exposed to fresh air. The reason is that he is accused of lying about his health in order to be out of the underground halls.

The other painful experience, but one that we got used to, is related to peeing and pooping. Our walls were full of soda bottles hanging down with threads full of urine. It was common to borrow another prisoner's bottle or to share a three or five liter jar among three-five prisoners at once. For any reason, peeing inside under's was not a problem. Pooping was hard but also not embarrassing.

When one is surprised by the need to poop, he shouts loudly "anybody have a plastic bag?" Those plastic bags, mostly enough to hold a kilo of sugar, are then given to him. He clears some space near his sleeping spot while those who sleep near him give him some space. He defecates in the plastic bag and ties it firmly. Then he puts it high on the roof of the under or throw it to outside through the opening of the door. When we wake up at 6am the next morning, we all carry our soda bottles full of pee and our poops in plastic bags and march to the hills where we pee and dump them there. Finding soda bottles is not as easy as it looks, hence one just pours the urine out and returns back with the bottle. It was common for someone to stop another prisoner and say "hey, may I add a little pee to your bottle?" or "Can you dump this urine for me since you are going out?" Since those pee bottles never get thrown away, they get very smelly day after day.

That takes time to get used to but it sure is disgusting at first. The idea of pooping in middle of hundreds of people and carry it in your hand next morning is outright disgusting. What helps is the cooperation from the prisoners who sleep near you especially. At some point, everyone suffers from some sort of an illness and thus, understands a prisoner in tough moments such as unexpected need to eliminate or vomit.

With all the setbacks, life under wasn't particularly hated. In fact, the under's were the most peaceful places at night because it is the only time of the day when there is a wall between us and the guards. It is the only time we can sit if we want to sit or walk around. It is the only place we are sure a guard will not come from behind and drop his beating rods on our backs. Sure, there were some guards who enjoyed disturbing that little peace we had in our under's. There were moments we were told to be totally silent. But the most unforgettable order was from a guard nicknamed Wedi Afar. We laughed after somebody told us a joke and he ordered: "You are prisoners. You are not supposed to laugh".

Sharing news was one of the most common things – real or fake/joke news (03 news). The death of military commanders was one of the well-received news. "Minus one! So close!" was the shortest way of expressing our joy over the death of the very people who played their part, directly or indirectly, in making our lives miserable. The hatred prisoners had towards EPLF became clear on January 2013, when some army people tried to overthrow the dictator out of power. Every prisoner was excited and hopeful. The death of military commanders was often good news. It is honestly sad to think about. We declared these people heroes at some stages of our lives but they became our arch enemies to the point we didn't feel sorry at their death. But then, we earned it. They made us hate them more than we ever loved them.

Public religious holidays were celebrated in each under. Members donate an amount regardless of their faith. Then biscuit and a few other items is bought and distributed to each member. The day is spent singing, dancing and telling jokes. In some occasions, we held singing and general knowledge competitions.

New Year and May 24 were the only public holidays when we eat meat prepared by the camp. New Year 2014 celebration started around 8pm in the newly built house Mendefera. Philemon was leading the celebration, which was going smoothly. Some of us were at work that afternoon and so weren't in full energy to follow the program. But he did wake us at midnight sharp to wish each other happy new year.

Almost all evenings had some jokes that belittle the government and the dictator in particular. The guards outside do hear some of the jokes but never minded. After all, they were victims themselves. Even though I have never heard any guard requesting for a joke to be retold, they never told us to quit it either. I can only imagine them laughing from the other end.

Songs were part of evening plans. Of all the songs, the one that stood out the most for me was "Zemen Tekeyrkani" by Yemane Barya. It is a song that describes the situation of each Eritrean, in prison or not and well loved. It is the only song that I heard in all the under's constantly.

Probably the hardest part of been a prisoner in Hashferay was the total isolation from family and friends. Any form of contact with the outside world was not allowed. Before the year 2012, families were allowed to visit prisoners on Saturday. But one Saturday, Tekle Manjus happened to be in the compound and saw a group of parents waiting. After he knew who they were, he gave an immediate order that family visitations be stopped completely and immediately. Of course, there is always an exception. If a prisoner knows someone who is powerful enough to approach the 'owners' of Command 1, they would certainly do so. I have seen it happen a few times and I can safely say that is like 0.1 percentages of the prisoners. The rest of us had to find a way to keep in touch with our families. And sure enough, ways did exist.

At the heart of each way found were the guards themselves. It might pose danger to them if their name is mentioned but without the guards, not a single letter, a pack of food and money would have found a way to us. We befriend one guard and make him our agent. There were some guards who would travel all the way to Asmara, meet a family, bring money and goods and slip it in at night or when we depart to the work place. Those guards would make equivalent to their monthly salary on each trip. Some guards would call families to come to Keren or Hagaz and meet them there.

I had two guards to help me get in touch with my family. The one would accept money, letters and all other stuff from Hagaz and bring me step by step. The other one would take orders and buy me things from Hagaz and bury them near the earth dam. The next day, when I go to work, I would bring my stuff in pieces, distribute it to other prisoners or in any other way and bring it in.

The other method of keeping in touch was through prisoners who were working at the bakery. The bakery, from which our bread was coming from, was located away from our compound, close to Hagaz. It had a snack bar at the front, too and so our families would come and meet one of the prisoners who work in the bakery. The prisoners come home every night and would bring stuff under the cover of darkness. Those prisoners were just as isolated as the rest of us to some extent and they had grown the habit of taking from the money or the items without first telling the intended prisoner. I was lucky enough for my agent, Angesom, was very trustworthy and gave me everything intact. There was also a time when, we the prisoners would go to the bakery to bring the breads every morning at 6. We would hide items in the middle of the bags and bring them back.

The other means was through the shepherds. Hashferay camp had goats and donkeys and elderly prisoners were looking after them. Those prisoners were trusted enough and had the chance to go as far as Hagaz in search of grass for the animals. Some parents and people would meet those shepherds and send us messages. My mother told me she had sent me some items and money through one of the men but I never got any. One day, at 6pm, a guard named Daniel was beating one of those shepherds. The man was crying and screaming like a little girl on the ground. Daniel, well known for his low-voice and quite nature, was very mean when he hits. He had the habit of putting his feet on the head and presses it down against the ground while turning the arm to one direction as it is a piece of thread. The shepherd was beaten up because he was found bringing some items to prisoners.

The administration knew all this tricks we used to be in touch with our family and took steps to cut it. They first brought donkey with its cart so the prisoners who work at the bakery would bring the bread on that cart every night, thus eliminating any other prisoner from going there at all. Then they created a separate sleeping space for the bakery prisoners, thus essentially cutting of ties with the rest of us. It was hard for a few days but since the guards were willing to help, new ways were found. We were not allowed to see the faces of our loved ones but we always were a step further in finding a way to keep in touch.

HEALTH ISSUES

Hashferay had a symbolic clinic with two nurses and their support aides (prisoners). One of the first things veteran prisoners tell new comers is this: 'No one cares about you here. You have to take care of yourself. But we also look after each other'. We play a huge role in the health issues of prisoners who are seriously ill. Often, we would be asked to donate any amount we can to someone so that things like sugar and milk could be provided.

That doesn't mean the members of the symbolic clinic (Mohammed, Andat and their prisoner assistants Samuel, Muktar and Awet) were in no way helpful. They were helpful. They cared. But they didn't have the resources at all. A prisoner would be given four pills for a severe headache because they can't afford to give all prisoners full pack. There were some medications that come in 5s or 10s for close to 1000 prisoners. They had no option but to reserve such pain killers to pregnant women and for unexpected cases.

The health station was a tiny hat outside the main compound, next to the entrance gate. Every Saturday, prisoners would be out for checkup at 8am. Someone who is unexpectedly sick or had an accident can visit on other days but only on cases considered major by their standard.

Doctors from Glass Military Hospital would come twice a month, usually on Wednesday mornings. Prisoners with severe cases were referred to the Doctors. When they come, the doctors bring with them medications to prisoners they have examined in their previous visit. I don't know for sure whose rule is it but the medications are carefully counted and come exactly in match to the previously examined prisoners. The doctors hand over the medications to the members of the clinic. The members subtract some amount from each pill and give the remaining to the intended prisoners. That way, they collect pills and syrups and use it for other prisoners.

Even with that trick, the clinic had severe shortage of basic pills, especially pain killers and anti-diarrhea pills. It also lacked any means of examination except the quick Malaria testing needle. They depended highly on physical examination. Some prisoners had an obviously major health issue. In such cases, the clinic had no any power except to suggest to Dimo's office for a transfer to Glas Military Hospital.

One of the most common illnesses among prisoners was arthritis, which was caused by the lack of Vitamin C. It starts off with a small pain in the feet then goes off to disabling someone from walking or walks with extra pain. The sight of prisoners using walking-sticks to walk was very common. The clinic was accepting 80-90 cases of arthritis per month. My main recollection of prisoners who suffered from this illness was their knees which becomes as tick and solid as glass itself. It was very hard to sleep next to them because every touch triggers pain.

Vitamin-C pills were unavailable at the clinic. The only thing the clinic can do to such prisoners was allowing them to eat Injera/bread and properly cooked lentil until they are really full. It had a positive outcome because the prisoners would soon show signs of improvement. Sadly, not all of the 80-90 prisoners were allowed to be on the mill plan because the clinic can't afford to do so. Hence, priority was given to those severely damaged prisoners.

Another common illness was diarrhea. It was an illness that terrified the administration as much as the prisoners. Before June 2013, prisoners had the option to wash their hands before eating food with soup powder provided by the administration. They really do take diarrhea seriously because it was powerful enough to spread through the prison overnight due to the inter-dependent lifestyle of prisoners. And the prisoners took steps to make sure they don't come close to the sickness because it was too strong to fight due to our weak immunity, lack of medication and poor diet. We shared the same water, ate from the same plate and slept with no space between us. It is truly surprising communicable diseases didn't destroy the prisoners.

The administration of the prison and the clinic had taken the step they could take in controlling the spread of diarrhea. They built a small tent to isolate the ill ones. The tent was so old to the point only one-fourth of it was protected from the sun. They were free from work and their food was generally separated from the main stream prisoners. They are as well isolated in sleeping arrangement. Some would sleep in one of the shoe cells, 2 by 4 wide, where there is no way for air to enter or leave. To aid them in the process of waste disposal, they bring with them a basket full of soil. Then they would go out on it and the next day, they would carry their waste to the hills outside. Those who sleep outside in the open air had their basket a bit distant from them. They would go at it now and then during the night and carry their basket full of poop out the next morning.

A prisoner can't come and say I need treatment for diarrhea. Instead, one the hours of peeing, he reports to the prisoners looking after the patients of the diarrhea tent and they come to check his poop on site. That visual check goes on until he goes out something they dim is free of diarrhea. The medication for diarrhea was one of the weakest brands, prolonging one's suffering unnecessarily.

On December 13, 2012, there was a diarrhea breakout in all prisoners after eating contaminated food. It happened after dinner, when the majority of the prisoners were put in the underground halls. The breakout came by surprise and took every hall by storm. The administration new they can't let everyone out at that time. So, they gave each hall a 50kg sack and hundreds of prisoners pooped one after the other in the sack in their respective under's. The incident repeated itself again on February 2014, in the newly built house of prisoners. The food was cooked at 10 and had been in the sun for nearly three hours. After we ate lunch and again dinner, things started piling up and every prisoner began going on plastic bags of any kind. The number increased dramatically and it was soon realized as a diarrhea breakout.

Keshi, Dimo and Tesfaldet came to the site and ordered we all be let out into the open air. A hole was quickly dug in one end of the fenced compound and everyone began going at it in pairs or in singles. That evening Tesfaldet ordered hall Mendefera to hold no more than 120 and hall Agordat no more than 80 prisoners at any given time. They got lemon for the garden of Hashferay located a few kilometers away. The next morning, everyone was forced to go to the river to wash and bath.

The administration is really terrified of a diarrhea breakout and they tend to react quickly but only when it happens.

I still recall the aftermath of suffering from diarrhea in Hashferay. One has to suffer from a serious weakness and dehydration. The clinic quickly releases cured ones out of its shelter, thereby exposing him to the tedious and labor intensive jobs around.

As a dump place, Hashferay had cases for Malaria. But luckily, the number of mosquitoes is few and thus its spread was not much of an issue.

Any other kind of illness wasn't really considered as an illness. The answers from the guards are rude but funny at the same time, especially to a side-watcher. One day a prisoner had painful tooth ache with a sign of swelling. When we were been gathered to head to work, he reported his case to the guard at hand. The guard replied 'You carry stones with your hands, not your teeth. Go!' One other day, a prisoner with wounds in his feet showed the soldier. The soldier looked at it and said 'You brought this injury from your home. It is not ours, just march forward.' Basically, internal pain barely matters for it is not visible to their naked eye. The few visible injuries that mattered always were the ones of complete disability.

With all the lack of medication and proper diet, one expects for the number of deaths to be higher. But thanks to God, it wasn't that much. In her first letter, my mother said 'The God in prisons is the mightiest one. You will be ok'. And I believed her especially after I got out. I witnessed only two deaths due to sickness in Hashferay. On December 09, 2013, Mr. Meshal of Agordat died of internal complications. He was around 70 years old and came to Hashferay from Under Tessenai with me. John Cena has severely wounded him in his testicles and the pain that started in May 2013 had stayed with him until the day dead. Mr. Meshal barely spoke and if he does, he would utter few Tigre words in a weak voice.

Families of dead people are not notified at all by the authorities. Instead, their families know of the death through prisoners who just left the prison. I am not sure if they bury the dead in one or different locations but I do know a few burial locations. On February 17, 2014, when Hagaz earth dam was getting upgraded on its right side, I saw one burial location. It was located between the mountains, where the river that heads towards Adi Ibrahim village heads. It had four poles around it with white rags hanging down in two of the poles as flags do.

I recalled then where they had buried the other prisoner. 5-6 months earlier, a prisoner in near dead state had come from Aderser prison. That day, we saw a group of Muslim men and a couple of Hashferay members gathered near the mountain. It made perfect sense he was buried in that spot; unrecognizable, unknown and forgotten.

SOLDIERS OF HASHFERAY

Time has proven multiple times how hard it is for anyone to be guard of others. That is especially hard in prisons where the guard and other members are there to do their job of locking prisoners up but they risk developing conflict and hatred with prisoners. Some conflicts and hatred are hard to let go and more than often, guards lose their life by prisoners who meet them in the free world.

Members of Hashferay, both the commanders and the low ranking guards, lead a stressful life. One day, aboy Efrem (Father Efrem) said it out loud: "We are the prisoners here, not you. You are getting punished for doing something wrong but we are getting punished more than you just because it is our job". He wasn't particularly wrong since they have to be on guard 24/7. For any sane and humanly person, it isn't easy to see anyone getting tortured and punished constantly. The only advantage the Hashferay members had was the location of the prison was on their side. It wasn't particularly easy to escape from. Their Command had put enormous effort to building an almost perfect prison.

But that doesn't save them from resting one bit. If they are not on guard, they have to welcome new prisoners on daily basis.

Some of the guards were mean and did enjoy torturing prisoners more than others. Granted, that number is few by all means. As time goes by and they get to interact with prisoners more and more, their heart does get touched and they tend to cool down slowly. As with everything in life, there were exceptions. There were guards who were kind from day 1. There were guards who became kind after a while. And there were guards who never became kind at all. The bottom line: they are the lords of the prison. Any member of the camp is entitled to doing almost anything he wants on a prisoner and get away with it. Some of the members forgot time changes and got carried away in making life of prisoners as miserable as possible. They forgot prisoners get freed at some point in life. Nobody knows who he or she meets in later life and that includes the very people who caused unbearable pain and punishment. Their lordship was temporary but few of them remember that.

There was a very mean and rude guard named Goitom Wedi Keshi. He was from Serha and he terrorized us big time. One soldier told us once that he says "The prisoners think they are educated and are well-experienced in life…I get to show them my power through beating" and he meant it. He enjoyed punishing us a lot. Goitom escaped to Ethiopia in June 2014. In the refugee camp, he wore a mask that covered his head and his face completely, in fear of been recognized by possible former prisoners. The hour came when his photo must be taken and so he had to take off his mask. Former prisoner John saw him and was shocked. He was calm but did ask him why he was super mean in Hashferay. His replied: "It is the place that makes one behave like that". While the reason was lame, he was lucky it was John, a calm, educated guy who recognized him.

The low ranking members/soldiers were mostly from Anseba region. As many new members of Command 1, almost all of them weren't properly trained soldiers. In fact, some were trained at the back of their village and got a gun. Thus they lack military discipline entirely. Looking at the life, we used to wonder "do this people have heads! How can they stay in this place?" I can't say for sure why many of them tolerated the place and stayed there. But for someone who don't want to worry about the future; for someone who want to escape the real challenges of life, it is a perfect place. There were members who look ill and sick when they come back from a break with their family. They gain their strength and health once they return back to Hashferay. It is hard to say the food is the main cause of the change but I personally believe in Hashferay, they hide from the typical life they lead in their village which included looking after goats or farming as well as dealing with family issues directly on a daily basis. In Hashferay, they had to look over prisoners and exercise some sort of power over them.

It can be said they, just like the rest of the nation, are forced to be soldiers and stay there as part of the national slavery program. I have no doubt that is true to some soldiers. But for many, it doesn't seem like it. You see, we run; we hide. That's what we do and that's what we are best at. How can one explain their habit of returning back from their homes after a few weeks, let alone disappear?

The low-ranking guards were the ones who suffer the most. They spend the entire day with us in the sun, in the dust and so forth and at night, when we sleep, they have to continue looking after us. And they didn't have enough to eat. I remember when I was sleeping outside in the open air; the guards would call Mussie the kitchen master, for raw bread. Their salary was the symbolic 600nacfa, from which certain amount is cut off for their daily food. Except three, all were addicted to smoking, tobacco and some were hardcore gamblers. I am sure none of them can live an ordinary life with what they remain with. That was evident in that some of them used to ask for cash from prisoners and even more humiliating, for a single cigarette because they can't afford it. It was an additional reason for them to help us get message from our family because they would take some amount from the money sent to us through them.

But with all that gloomy life, their number barely changed. For reasons we never understood, many of them did stay there.

Now let me introduce you to some of them.

Brig. General Tekle Manjus

We use to call him Ewir (blind) because his left eye was blind. At that time, he was a Brig. General and commander of Command 1. He was transferred to Major General and became commander of Command 2. As the top man in Command 1, Manjus had a direct effect on all that happens in Hashferay prison. Known for his merciless nature and arrogance, he used to stop by Hashferay now and then but barely came close to prisoners. His observation was done from a distance. In fact, he entered the main compound of prisoners just once. That day, all prisoners were gathered at the center in a small square with seven guards surrounding us. He stood near the kitchen; about 200m away and just looked at us for about five minute. No one was explaining to him anything; just observing. The most demeaning part of his visit wasn't that however; we were the last item in his item of interest that day. First, he went through the compound, observing the trees and water tank where they were explaining to him things. After he was done with everything, he turned his head to us and pretended to be interested. He left in silence. There was no prisoner who didn't know his story; his hard heart. None of us expected him to say something good, if anything at all. History reveals that each such visit brings with it a negative change in the lives of prisoners. That visit didn't change anything, negative or positive.

On March the 12th, 2014, high ranking commanders of Command 1 lead by Brig. General Liqe visited the earth dam we built. The visit fitted the rumor that Blind Tekle was leaving Command 1 and was getting replaced by Wedi Liqe. Wedi Liqe was more or less new to Hashferay.

But those who knew him, especially former members of Division 23 in the years between 1998 and 2000 swore by his kindness. Everyone knew at heart there is no one worse than Tekle Manjus as far as the lives of the youth and prisoners was concerned (I said that to a veteran soldier there and he smiled "what about the big Satan?" in reference to the dictator in power). I didn't get to try the new administration at all to give my judgment. There was change in Hashferay but I doubt it was because of the transfer of Manjus alone. The notorious and well-feared Major General Philipos became Minister of Defense. They are sworn enemies and upon becoming commander of Manjus, Philipos ordered Special Forces to release 451 prisoners from Hashferay to prisons of their army units in July 2014. Though he did it to show his power over Manjus, it was good for the prisoners who had seen their life going nowhere in the arms of Command 1. Many prisoners in shoe were sent to military training camps. In fact, towards the end of 2014, only a few of the veteran prisoners remained, including my dear friend Bereket and the others related to the immigration scandal.

I can imagine the order to release prisoners came as a shock to the commanders of Hashferay. We built their prison from the ground up and they have endless labor-demanding projects. But there is someone more powerful than the powerful one. Maj. Gen Philipos was that one for the officers of Command 1.

Bashay Asfaha (Dimo)

Bashay is in fact his real name (those of you who don't know its meaning; Bashay is an honorary rank/title given typically to an elder. It is a prefix to a person's first name). But he is known by his nick name Dimo, which means dumb. His nick name was very well suited and appropriate for him. Truly, he is dumb! Dimo's home was in Barentu and he had spent most of his professional life as administrator of prisons. Before he came to Hashferay, he was the head of Prima Country (Barentu) and Aderser (Forto Sawa) prisons.

Gaining job experience makes normal people smarter and better. Not for Dimo. From time to time, he was becoming dumber and dumber, not to mention arrogant. It is extremely hard to understand how the ignorant and arrogant Dimo climbed up the hierarchy to his high position. He didn't only lack management skills but he had no respect for the human soul, especially those under him. That included all soldiers and the guards under him. One guard once told us that Dimo never acknowledges their existence and don't greet them at all.

Dimo has a well-known hatred of prisoners and made no effort to simplify their life at all. There are many facts one can bring to show his actions that made our lives harder and harder.

In 2013, there were at least 10 HIV positive prisoners. They were getting weaker and weaker because they haven't checked their CD4 and followed their medication for nearly seven months. They asked formally to be taken to Keren Hospital for test and medication. Dimo rejected their plea with lame excuses like "there is no car to take you to Keren Hospital", "We don't have fuel for the car" etc. That went on for months and at last they told him in clear words "our life is hanging in your hands" and then he decided to send him to Keren Hospital with five guards. The funny thing was that Dimo had a mistress in Glass hospital. He had to visit her on the car he was using as an excuse now and then or send the car to her on her request.

In a related issue, there were prisoners whose illness was too complicated to handle for the medics of Hashferay. In that case, they would refer the prisoner to Glass military hospital. Dimo must approve such a referral and he never wanted to do so. In fact, he was rejecting such demands right away. Those once he did approve were near death. In fact, the doctors in Glass hospital used to say of each new patient they get "You brought a corpse again". But it never mattered to Dimo. Hashferay follows one law that is not written on papers but in their heads: the death of a prisoner doesn't matter; escape of a prisoner does.

Dimo was well known for his history of not granting mercy to prisoners. Pretty much all prisons had the tradition of showing mercy to prisoners on May 24 and New Year. No prison has done such a thing under the management of Dimo. That truth did keep us sane to some extent because we can't expect a gift from Dimo on those days at all and simply move on.

It is said that his master Tekle Manjus said once "I don't want to see elders at all". But Dimo interfered and said "these elders are smugglers who smuggled people multiple times. We can't let them go" and blocked their chance of been free. I can understand why he and other officials wouldn't wish to free young prisoners but why keep an 80-90 year old man who doesn't do a damn thing except sit down the whole day and night? The truth is they are not their fathers and grandfathers.

May be you are wondering why I said "not their sons, not fathers" again. You are not mistaken. The thing is even the cruel Dimo was soft towards prisoners he was connected with somehow. There were a group of prisoners caught in relation to forged travel documents. It was a serious matter for it involved escaping the country too. One of the prisoner's (Alex) father was a lawyer (if memory serves right, his name was Habte), who got strong connections with government and army officials. Somehow, he connected with Dimo and Dimo called Alex to his office for a private talk. He acted like a father and advised him to be a good young man. He then freed him alone from his accomplices. That was just an example of the deep corruption and discrimination that runs within Hashferay Camp and once again, I was glad Alex was freed at all costs.

November 19, 2013 was a unique day in the history of Dimo. It was the first time he got a face to face meeting with the prisoners at a close range. He disgusted us clearly to the point that he wouldn't say a word to us even when we are close; instead he would order a nearby guard or soldier to order us to do what he wants. That day, everyone except the prisoners who are members of Command 1, was gathered at the center. The guards surrounded us and Dimo and Keshi were at the front. He was forced to conduct the meeting because that week, prisoners had escaped from Bidho Prison in Asmara. It was why his entire speech was mainly about escaping: "You are getting punished according to your crimes. Trying to escape is a second crime. If anyone tries to escape, we will shoot him!" He continued with the usual propaganda of EPLF and the army commanders that had accompanied us all through the years: "We will build a library for you. We can get you enough food and water. We will build a better clinic just for you...." However, not the entire meeting was a lie. When he opened his speech, he said "Don't ask about mercy and knowing the length of your sentences." He ignored any question that remotely related to those crucial questions.

There was a 12 year old kid named Semir from Keren seated in front of him. He raised him up and said "It is a shame this kid tried to cross the border! Can you imagine jailing this kid? Why would he escape?" He forgot the underage and the elders sitting in front of him were there by the very policies he supports. Ironically, though, they do guide their own kids escape the country to a better land because they know the system they built is not suitable for the future of the people.

He had given us the chance to ask questions in the end. None of the questions asked were really crucial but I do recall a comment given by a 70-something father: "Today you did a good job! We never knew our administrator". Dumb Dimo probably had no head that can decode and understand the insult in that message but it was pretty good mock.

Semere Fessahaye (Keshi)

Semere, known as Keshi ('priest'), was from the Qohain region of Eritrea and the second ranking official after Dimo. Towards the end of 2013, his rank was raised to Battalion leader. I didn't get concrete information regarding his joining of the army; some say he joined the army in 1990 while others say he was with the first round (1994) trainees. Omer, a prisoner from Begu, was with Keshi in the Ethio-Eri war in 2000 and told me that Keshi got wounded in his feet and it was why his right leg limbs background a little as he walks.

Keshi was a true soldier in all sense. He was considerably fair in this handling of prisoner cases. He never wanted to be found guilty and at fault. Though some would disagree, I personally found him to be disciplined too. Some of his men would harm prisoners and a smart prisoner would go straight to Keshi for justice. He would bring both parties face to face right in front of him and let them talk one after another and then decide almost always in favor of prisoners.

Another notable feature of Keshi was his complete disregard for a prisoners' tribe, religion or status. He was quite honest in all his talks and says things straight out. One of the things he constantly repeated to his soldiers was "We know you guys bring money and items to the prisoners. Either give them everything entirely or don't bring any to them". That's because prisoners would complain to him about money or items stolen by one of his men.

Just like any other soldier/guard, Keshi used to bring message to prisoners from his village or those who know him. But he wasn't reluctant to punish those he found bringing items to prisoners as a reminder that they are not allowed to do so and of course, that his higher rank excludes him from the rule.

With all his military-suited nature, Keshi had a big flaw that overshadowed all his positive qualities. That flaw was his disregard for the mental and physical state of prisoners. He thinks of prisoners as robots who never get tired at all. He had no mercy as far as work is concerned. But his worst spot was his inability to be satisfied with completed works. It was incredibly hard to satisfy him, hence we would work and strive an extra mile to gain his approval. It was why we hated him. The presence of Keshi in Hashferay camp often disrupts the compound because he creates jobs out of the blue. He clearly hated to see prisoners in a happy and relaxed mood. It is hard to say why such a view would disturb him but maybe, just maybe, he also believes prisoners shouldn't laugh?

Keshi generally followed military rules. He barely hit anyone with stick or so. But even then, he would really ask prisoners a few questions before he moves to punishment. His choice of punishment was mostly physical; sitting down and raising up every second until the knees start to hurt. But that nature of his came at a price. He was smart enough to have learned from his mistake. He was in Aderser prison before he was transferred to Hashferay. One day, he joined forces with Wedi-Fichel and tortured a prisoner and left him almost dead. The prisoner was taken to Mohammed, the medic who insisted they sign a document stating the prisoner come to him in the state he was in. They refused because it would imply responsibility. The prisoner dead as a result of the torture and lack of proper medical care. While Wedi-Fichel continued that path of violence, Keshi pulled back and used mainly words to terrorize prisoners.

Keshi did struggle to make his men disciplined. And he had failed entirely.

Aboy Efrem

Aboy means father. We called him Aboy Efrem out of respect for his fatherly love and respect to prisoners even though he was young. Aboy Efrem was from Bariesa, near Omhajer and he was after Keshi in rank. He was very well known and loved by prisoners because he was the only one who saw past our current crime and looked at us as his sons, brothers, fathers and daughters. He was a frequent user of the term "my sons" and often would use prisoner's first name as opposed to the insulting "you!" Having Aboy Efrem in the work place was such a blessing because he was calm and gets happy at what we did at the end of the day. He would even throw the exceptionally rare word: thank you! There were many, many days his kindness was shown but let me share with you one that I remember dearly.

We were at labor intensive work the whole day. So when we finally came to the compound at 5, we were hungry and tired. Rain started falling just when we started making queues to take our dinner. Rain is one of the most perfect cover-ups for prisoners who want to escape and so, it is a prison's night mare. All the soldiers got into the compound and started pushing us back into our underground halls. It was decided we wouldn't have dinner that night. It meant we would go without eating the whole night and go to work until 10am the next day with an empty stomach.

Aboy Efrem came to the compound and said "Those kids are not going to die of hunger. Take the food to their hall's". The guards opposed it but they eventually caved in to his firm order and gave us our daily bread.

Issais Wedi-Fichel

If "who is the most hated member of Hashferay?" was asked, the answer would be definitely Issais Wedi-Fichel. He was the assistant of 2ND platoon and known for his ambition of more power and deep hatred of prisoners. He was a kiss-ass and would make extra effort to be liked by Aboy Efrem, Keshi and Dimo. Wedi Fichel was previously member of Division 37 and was member of Command 1's sport team.

Wedi-Fichel had hands deeply washed with crime and wrongdoing. It is probably for this reason he barely leaves Hashferay even though his family was in Asmara. The soldiers were pretty fine with each other but even they were sick of him. One afternoon, Saleh Zebra and Mokie were standing by the gate when Wedi-Fichel appeared at a distance. Then Mokie said "When did the snitch come back?" Wedi-Fichel was involved in a physical fight with another soldier named Hilal. The cause of the hatred was that he was, as Mokie said, a snitch. But he failed to impress

Keshi and so the higher rank he dreamt of deeply never came to pass (as far as I know).

The stupidity and crime of Wedi-Fichel is the biggest one in Hashferay. On August 28, 2013, some smugglers from the shoe cells attempted to escape. It was a more or less failed attempt but a moment for Wedi-Fichel to shine in front of his masters. He was actively chasing the escapees and he was almost the only one who was seen moving from corner to corner in the compound. He had the perfect excuse to torture those caught ones to the pain of disbelief. He targeted Wedi-Keshi and Kubrom, the main suspects of the escape attempts and beat them to the point Kubrom, a full grown man, began screaming like a little girl at the torture falling on him. Around 6pm, Wedi-Fichel was seen wondering the shoes with a bunch of plastics in his hands. And he blocked the only air-holes the shoes had with the plastic he brought. That combined with hunger led to the death of Kubrom in September 8, 2013. It was rumored the order to block the shoes completely from fresh air came directly from Tekle Manjus but I am a living witness that only Wedi-Fichel, from the soldiers, did the order from whoever it came from, including himself.

In another occasion, Wedi-Fichel had his eyes set on one smuggler jailed in one of the shoes. He was set to making his already miserable life more miserable. So, he would beat him, insult him and spit on him every chance he got. The prisoner was naturally weak, as all shoe prisoners were and once, he felt sick. That didn't stop Wedi-Fichel from slowing down. On the last day the prisoner dead, Wedi-Fichel kicked him down the stairs to the shoe and he crushed his head as he rolled down. Those were his last breath and Wedi-Fichel got what he wanted. No one held him responsible because no one has the right to enquire. He can bring any reason to justify his actions, including denying he had anything to do with the death. The truth is he just followed the law: "Death of a prisoner is not questionable; an escape is".

His hatred was stronger towards smugglers. I bet he would have built a much deeper pit-hole to cage them in if he had the power to do so. It is hard to say where that hatred emerged from. And it is even harder to understand why, especially when his past is looked after. Wedi-Fichel has a brother who fled Eritrea to Sudan then to Israel. Unfortunately, before he reached Israel, he was kidnapped in the Sinai dessert by human traffickers. His family was asked ransom money that was far beyond their ability to pay. Wedi-Fichel was petitioning members of Command 1, including Hashferay to donate any amount they can. Luckily, he got enough and his brother was freed to Israel. Now, Wedi-Fichel swears by his brother's will to help him at least money wise. Could his anger be a result of what happened to his brother in the Sinai dessert because there were many times smugglers would sell escapees for more money? His brother escaped for a better future. How was Wedi-Fichel so mean to the rest of us who wanted the same thing as his brother?

Wedi-Fichel had exceptional stupidity that was based on his desire to be feared and seen as someone who follows the law strictly. One morning, he went with 12 prisoners to bring bread from the bakery. Civilians are allowed to wonder within the walking distance of the bakery shop and that morning, a desperate mother was there in search of someone to send her message to her son. Fortunately, her son was one of the prisoners on duty that morning. Her son was at the front, Wedi-Fichel was at the back with his gun. The prisoner saw his mother and thought for a second. If he asks Wedi Fichel for permission to say hi to his mother, he will surely reject it. Knowing that, the prisoner put down the sack of bread on his head and run to his mother. Wedi-Fichel began shouting: 'Get back! Get back!' The son had kissed his mom and she slipped him some money but nothing more. Wedi-Fichel reached them and pulled the mother away from him with force. He took the money away from the prisoner and threw it at the mother. Then he kicked and insulted him in front of his mother, who begged and begged for mercy. Once they arrive to the compound, Wedi-Fichel had the pleasure of tying the prisoner in iron cuffs under the sun. The prisoner was highly appreciated by the rest of us. He did come to Hashferay to be jailed. But to be jailed after seeing and kissing your mother is such a huge blessing that anyone would gladly do it no more the price. Around 11am, Mahmud was wondering the compound and stopped by the prisoner. After learning what happened, he loosened the chains but can't free him. Only the soldier/guard who chained a prisoner can undo it.

Wedi-Fichel was one of the soldiers known for stealing money he promised to deliver to us from our parents. He got away because no-one dared to report him. He was mean as he is and we knew the hell he will put us through if we report him to Keshi. May be I am diving into his personal life but Wedi-Fichel was insane with women. He took pride in his ability to seduce any girl he wants and say it out loud: "there is no woman I wouldn't have sex with". There was a mentally sick woman who walks the streets of the Tessenai with a baby in her hand. Regardless of the truth, he used to tell his friends with so much pride that he had sex with her. He had a baby out of wedlock when he was stationed in Aderser prison. During my time in Hashferay, he was seeing a bar girl in the nearby town of Hagaz. Prisoners from Hagaz long suspected she was HIV positive. One thing was true: he was in conflict with her because she had a baby and he denied it was his.

There were prisoners who were his neighbors in Asmara but he barely acknowledged their very existence. For reasons known to them, they didn't expect the tiniest smile from him either.

By all means, Wedi-Fichel had a negative image in all prisoners of Hashferay. He was equally hated by the soldiers, who definitely would give him up in times of trouble.

Ismael

One of the soldiers known by "tawla" or "terew", Ismael had many characteristics of a soldier. He was from the village Asmat and known for his unchanging views on any subject matter. He quickly jumped to rank of assistant of first platoon because of his commitment in the service. He barely went home and if he does, he would return back on time. In the end, he had the same rank with Wedi-Fichel, who had been in the army for more than a decade.

Just like Keshi, Ismael don't discriminate based upon religion or ethnic. He looks at everyone the same way, even though some prisoners had a language advantage at least. It is why everyone, including those he knew very well, would not expect a special treatment at all. He seemed to have followed the footsteps of Keshi in his understanding of justice too. Ismael was quite fair in dealing with cases of prisoners in conflict and often brings the two parties face to face and gives each one equal space and chance. Basically, Ismael have no favorite prisoner. But because of his strict rules and quite unforgiving nature, Ismael was not anybody's favorite either.

Often he was too bored, lazy and arrogant to do physical harm. But if he does hold grudge, he causes serious injuries that can continue after prison time. His favorite spot was the muscular joints and prefers to use his hard as rock stick. One of his severely punished victims was Adil, a prisoner with mental issues (though some used to say he was faking it). One day, everyone was told to sit down and Adil was standing and walking. Suddenly, Ismael came from the back and tapped him. Adil turned back and gave Ismael a hard punch on the face, just below the left eye and he fall down. Nearby prisoners separated them. At that time, Ismael wanted to hit him but Keshi was around and ordered Ismael not to touch him but put on iron handcuffs in the sun.

After we were dispersed, Ismael came with his rod and started beating Adil in his joints. We were close and were able to hear the sound of the stick falling on Adil's bones. Adil was tied in "helicopter" style, barely able to move except to scream. He was saying "please, I am sorry, I am sorry". That day Adil was terrified more than ever and the state of his mind deteriorated significantly that day and after.

Ismael was a shepherd when he was in Asmat. He later started digging gold in the nearby mountains and was making enough cash. But he had a serious drinking problem that emptied his pocket severely. He was a regular at a bar called Roma, which earned him the nick name Wedi Roma ("Son of Roma"). One day, he was found on the mountains of Asmat by a Command 1 soldier nick named Shilu. Shilu became a prisoner in Hashferay for helping some youngsters escape the country. Shilu used to complain about the life of Command 1 soldiers so much but he wasn't reluctant to put another young into the life he hated so much. That action reminds me of a post I read in Facebook long ago: "The worst enemy of an Eritrean is an Eritrean".

I left Ismael behind been one of the most feared soldiers. But I admit he was becoming better from time to time, mostly because of the extended interaction with prisoners. I heard, after I left Eritrea, that he became much better and cooperative after he saw more prisoners leaving Hashferay. He was obviously concerned what could happen to him if one of those hundreds of prisoners found him outside.

Mahmud (Wedi Nakfa)

Known for his very low and soft voice and the ear phones he never put out of his ears, Mahmud was the most educated one from all the soldiers. Born and raised in Nakfa, he came to Hashferay hoping to be in the offices. But he ended up been an ordinary soldier/guard just like the others. Mahmud was very decisive, confident and never feared any of his masters. We liked him primarily because he never does anything to please Keshi or anyone else for that matter. He didn't want to hurt prisoners though sometimes he took senseless decisions. There were rumors he shows favor to prisoners from Nakfa or the Tigre ethnic but I personally have never seen that happen. No one feared him but respected him. He was one of the guards on board with us when we were finally transferred from Hashferay to Adi Abeto and he did choke when we said good bye.

There were other soldiers. Drar, Fitwi, Tesfai, Gide, Fish and all members of division 63 were very much loved and respected. Saleh (Zebra) was known for his sly mind and bitter tongue and one of the most hated guards.

MOST FAMOUS PRISONERS

Hashferay is allowed to jail anyone, including army commanders with rank as high as a colonel. As told before, there were all kinds of prisoners, from all walks of life. Some cases were purely civilian in their nature (such as the theft, fights) but the all-powerful Hashferay prison took their matters and treated them in a military compound. Others included smugglers, escapees, religious related, human traffickers and other minor crimes.

At one point, one colonel active on duty in Ministry of Defense was captured and brought to Hashferay (I forgot his name but it is either Haile or Goitom). On the first day, he looked around and was surprised at the about 80-100 children aged as young as 10. Whether he was pretending not to know or not, he said with a great surprise and believable tone: "What is this?! It exists for real?" I would have loved to talk about each prisoner there but it is not practical so let me just share with you the most well-known prisoners or prisoners whose cases amaze me.

Colonel Amn Idriss Abu Taweela (Tewil)

The mention of that name sends shivers in the Gash Barka zone, especially the town of Tessenai and those around. Colonel Tewil was head of the National Security Agency in Gash Barka zone with his office stationed in Tessenai. He is one of the military people with one of the darkest picture in the mind of the people. He is hailed as been the one who crushed the so called "5th rank" opposition operating in Gash Barka region. But he had left a dark spot in the hearts of the civilians and residents. He was extremely arrogant and cruel to the point he had torture shoe under his residential housing. He is also the first one to order the death of smugglers by a firing squad. He was present in person as two smugglers were shot in person in Tessenai, which was a way to scare the people and other possible smugglers.

Tessenai was also office to the then Commander of Border Control Brig. General Tekle Manjus. They were like sworn enemies and barely tolerated each other for reason I don't know. Under the leadership of dictator Issais, every commander gets to shine high and above for a set period of time, only to fall down and be replaced by another favorite. As such, National Security was once at the top and the most powerful sector. They had terrorized the nation and its agents had the absolute power to do anything they want and get away with it. In a word, they were untouchable and above the law. Then the turn of Tekle Manjus to rise to the top as commander of Command 1 arrived and he ruled with iron feast and his agents successfully continued the legend left by national security agents. Eventually, the National Security was overshadowed and remained more or less symbolic as all security tasks seemed to have been handled by Command 1. That meant, for the first time, Manjus had an edge over the weakened Tewil. Tewil is very stubborn as a person and drunk with arrogance. It was obvious he took the rise of Manjus very hard. And it wasn't hard to imagine Manjus would act on Tewil if he finds the slightest excuse. And that excuse came in 2010.

One of Tewil's nephews was doing contraband business between Sudan and Eritrea. In one of his trips, he was ordered to stop for check up by armed police who check for contraband items. He disobeyed and drove past their gate and a chase started. After he refused to stop, they had no choice but to start firing. As they were closing in the town of Tessenai, a shot aimed at the car found its way to Tewil's nephew and he dead instantly. That raised a huge conflict between the family of Tewil and the police. The family blamed police saying the killing was targeted, while police soldiers stated they aimed the car but lost and killed him. The family obviously felt superior and untouchable for they have the strongman Tewil on their side. Things took ugly turn when the family started attacking the police and the police station with stones demanding the person who fired the shot to be handed to them.

Tekle Manjus was watching from side and soon, he sent his men to arrest Tewil on the ground of exploiting his power to support his family and turn things ethnical and tribal. He also jailed Tewil's brother Ibrahim along with him and both were taken to Aderser prison. Tewil was transferred to Hashferay in 2012 while his brother Ibrahim remained in Aderser, leading a comfortable life in a prison known for its complete isolation, hunger and lack of anything basic.

When he was brought to Hashferay first, he was taken to Tesfaldet for investigation. He slapped Tesfaldet on the right cheek, saying "I am a Colonel. Who are you to question me?" As a rule, a Colonel can be questioned only by an equal or higher ranking official. As such, the secretary of the security section of Command 1 Colonel Yonas took the charge and questioned Tewil in Hashferay. After a few days, he was told he is free to go. But Tewil said "Let the man who ordered my arrest come in person and tell me I am free". He was referring to Manjus, who didn't even acknowledge his existence in Hashferay prison.

The last time I enquired about him was September 2014 and he was still there, in one of the shoes but like a free man. He wasn't part of the ordinary life. Every morning, he was given 20liter of water to wash in a private bath built for him. He had a bed and his door is always open though he barely left his shoe. The two platoons would take turn in giving him his daily food.

Wedi Guret

One of the most well-known and respected singers of Tigre music, Wedi-Guret was jailed in the biggest and arguably the most comfortable shoe: Agordat. Known for his long and strong lyrics, Wedi-Guret was caught on January 21, 2013. Everyone was making calls on that day for there was a coup of attempt by members of the armed forces. And Wedi-Guret called his friend and collogue Tesfai Qanta in Asmara to enquire about what was happening. Qanta told him what everybody was seeing and hearing that morning. Wedi-Guret was happy like the majority of the people. But once he got drunk, he began expressing his happiness in public. He said out loud "It is all over now! You have nothing!" and members of Command 1 Security Unit of Keren caught him and jailed him. They also caught Tesfai Qanta and they accused them of knowing about the coup before it happened. They didn't have any evidence nor there seems to be any relationship except Wedi-Guret's over excitement of that day's incidence.

Upon arrival to Hashferay, Wedi Guret was placed and remained in Agordat while Tesfai Qanta was in the regular under's and was freed on January 2014. Wedi-Guret was generally respected by the soldiers (most of them were Tigre) but there was no favor they can show him at all but no one dared to put a finger on him no matter what. At one point, he was stunk by scorpion and they let him out after it got worse. He was placed alone in the tent used by prisoners suffering from diarrhea. That day, money was gathered from prisoners by prisoners to buy date fruit, milk, sugar and so forth for him.

Mensur Wedi Keren

One of the cancers of the city of Keren, Mensur was a very well-known snitch of Command 1, who was responsible for jailing many of its youth daily and intentionally. Many of the youth he jailed were young people he knew personally and for no major reason. I feel I am honoring him by giving him a sub-title of his own in this book but he got to be told about so that everyone can know him. Mensur, black-skinned with a big-beer-belly, was officially demobilized from the defense forces. He joined the snitches in Keren, led then by Abdu, by giving them tips they didn't send him to collect but eventually got their interest and he joined them. Just like many Command 1 agents, he had no formal introduction, let alone training and experience, in the field of intelligence. Actually, what he was doing didn't require anything all practically. Because the only thing he was assigned to do was eaves-drop on people and bring anyone thinking of escaping the country, speak ill of the dictator and his puppies and anything else they dim is not good. Mensur took his job as a national security agent and wanted to be feared. He did get feared to some extent. He had the ambition of appearing as a high-ranking security agent with secrets. Of course, everyone in Keren knew he was nothing beyond an eves-dropper. But he had power. He had the security unit on his side. Some prisoners from Keren used to tell us how his arrival to a bar would trigger others to leave almost instantly. He had the habit of inputting ideas (such as escape the country) into the heads of his victims and led them to jail straight forward. He had no power to torture and beat anyone or to release them free. But he used to assure the beaters and torturers that he would be held responsible for anything that can happen during the beating as long as it is done for the information he swears is "there". That way, he had played direct role in the torture of many innocent citizens as well as excessive force on the ones with a little black dot.

When he arrived to Hashferay, prisoners from Keren and the surrounding villages wanted to kill him. His arrival was a perfect example of the power of law and fear of punishment because they knew anything they do to him will back fire at them fiercely. On May 5, 2013, he was sleeping in Under Tessenai. At night, they peed on his water bottle and left it there for him to drink from. He had no friends in the under and the only option he had was to report the incidence to the guards in the morning.

The guards told prisoners in Under Tessenai to bring out the person who did it but no one stood up nor did they give him up. Though I didn't personally know who did it for I was sleeping in Under Titanic by then, I have no doubt they all knew who did it. They were scheduled for punishment after the mid-day count when the sun is the strongest, they are tired from the morning work hour and would go back to work at 2pm, right after they finish their punishment. It was better to be punished than to reveal the person(s) who peed in his water jar. It was the only way they can pay him back for his evil deeds and it isn't enough by all standards. As a result, everyone who sleeps in under Tessenai was punished from 12:30 to 1:45 and went to severe work at 2pm.

In other occasions, he had a bit of verbal exchange with a guy named Munir, who he jailed from Keren. Munir was jailed without any crime and he had a lot of anger inside him. So he lost control of his anger and hit Mensur with a stone at the back of his head and Mensur bleed. That threw Munir to shoe for the next 2 months. Munir used to work in the water distribution section and was sleeping outside in the open air. After he got of shoes, he was kicked out all jobs and made to sleep in Under Nakfa. Let me tell you why and how Munir was in Hashferay. He was working in a multi-media shop in Keren. One day, a girl came to his colleague in the shop and asked him if he knows any smugglers to Sudan. "I don't know. Ask Munir, may be he knows" So she turned to Munir and asked him the same thing, to which he replied he had no idea. She left them alone and found smugglers on her own. Unfortunately, she got caught and she was asked who she has enquired about escaping to Sudan and she told of the brief conversation she had with Munir and his colleague.

They were caught and Munir was especially targeted: 'If you had no hand in the business, your friend wouldn't have told her to ask you'. Munir resisted the allegations but remained in prison for more than a year.

Mensur used to brag about his activities and his role in "cleaning-up" Keren inside-out even after he was jailed with the very people whose lives he destroyed. "I was so close to cleaning Keren from smugglers, money launders, abortionists, and druggists...I still have the list of names of the remaining ones. They will see what I will do once I am out." What he forgot is everyone had the chance to be out as himself. Mensur had survived a murder attempt once but he was too caught up in his arrogance that he thinks the next won't be a success.

Mensur was captured in relation to bribe. One smuggler paid him 10,000.00Nfa and Mensur released him. When he got caught, he turned his back to Mensur and brought him down with him. Mensur was released in April 2014. Since he had no place in the society, am sure he at least would try to go back to his job as a snitch.

Yonatan and Senai

As Mensur was the cancer of Keren, Yonatan and Senai were the cancer of Asmara working for Idirs under Division 59 of Command 1. They were deeply isolated when they came to Hashferay towards the end of 2013. They have the same background but for the sake of easy reading, let me introduce you with them one by one.

Senai Redie, aged around 30, was supposed to go to Sawa military training with the 16th round in 2002 but delayed it somehow and went with 25th round instead. His home was around Muler Car Wash, near University of Asmara. As a kid, he was famous around the neighborhood for stealing from houses around and nearby places. The habit of stealing was stuck with him and he was jailed for stealing at some point as an adult. Senai, a heavy smoker, was a guard at Ministry of Information under Division 59 before he became an eves-dropper for Idirs.

I became close with Senai after we met at the diarrhea tent. He was open about his job; in fact he was very proud and satisfied with every single operation he was a part of. "They were doing their job; I was doing mine". One evening, he whispered "Our job could block marriage. It is embarrassing to be known and called an ear-ring" (ear-ring is an insult used to refer to people like Senai who report people now and then and were badly hated). Of course, he didn't mean it. He was gaining our friendship and trust. With his name out there, Senai had no real place in the society. It was obvious he would be back to his old job the meant he gets out of Hashferay. It was why I and another prisoner Sami gave him wrong phone numbers when he asked for our numbers. Senai had many roles in the capture and jailing of many youths, with his most notable role related to the immigration case.

Yonatan, recognized by his big beer belly, became puppy of Idirs after he got out of Sembel Correctional Facility where he was jailed for theft. At some point, he had taken over the role of torture and beating, which apparently is a higher rank. He was fierce in his beating and wants to leave memory and assure his dominance by constantly repeating the words "Do you know who I am? My name is Yonatan! I am Yonatan!"

Yonatan and Senai were captured because of bribe and treason. Prior to their capture, they were on a mission to capture a smuggler who was using a motorized-boat to smuggle people to Yemen. They had an idea about him but they wanted to capture the boat too. To accomplish the task, Yonatan approached the smuggler as someone who wants to escape to Yemen and the undercover operation started. He was believed and was told to wait for the day of departure. But at some point, Yonatan told the smuggler he was been wanted by Idirs. He accepted 10,000.00nfa for his info and the smuggler disappeared. The disappearance was particularly disappointing to Idirs because the operation seemed on its last stage. He asked Senai how he escaped but Senai had no idea. He tried Yonatan's number, which was locked.

Suddenly, the smuggler called Idirs on his mobile phone and insulted him and told him the truth. Idirs dialed and redialed Yonatan's number until he answered it. Yonatan told him he was in Massawa as part of the operation. Then Idirs called Senai and said "Why is Yonatan alone in Massawa? Why aren't you with him?" It was a trick question to test Senai's part in what Idirs just learned. Senai seemed to have known because he revealed Yonatan's lie right away. "No, he is in Asmara" and they went together to see Yonatan having a good time at a bar.

Before the smuggler escaped, Senai had confided in Idirs that he is not feeling good about the operation and they should just go ahead and arrest the smuggler even at the risk of never capturing the boat. But Idirs badly wanted to capture the motorized-boat for they weren't sure if it was in Eritrea or Yemen. Soon after that Idirs arrested both Yonatan and Senai. Idirs believed Senai had nothing to do with it but Yonatan insisted that Senai also had a hand, so Idirs had no option but to lock Senai too. They were questioned, without physical violence, in Asmara. The questioning there was just for Yonatan to admit Senai's innocence, but he insisted Senai knew. When they drove to Hashferay on Saturday, Idirs had said: "Tell me the truth and I will take you back with me". But they didn't change their words. Then Idirs told Yonatan to free Senai, to which he replied "He had hand in it. Why should he be freed alone?" and that led both of them to the gates of Hashferay as official prisoners.

When coming from Asmara, Yonatan and Senai didn't exchange any words. But once they were off the bus to enter the gate, Senai turned to Yonatan and said "Listen, we are going to a compound of people we put to jail. Let's not be a laughingstock, okay? Let's hide our differences and anger towards each other and pretend to be at peace?" Yonatan realized the power in Senai's word and agreed. They walked into the punishing eyes of us, walking side by side, smoking their cigarette, exchanging words. Until Senai told me all this, I never would have imagined they were not friends anymore. Their interaction was purely artificial.

Prisoners from Asmara immediately recognized them when they walked in. Soon, their identity circulated to everyone else and as they expected, every eye punished them and they were isolated. Yonatan was particularly stressed, walking up and down, smoking non-stop. Senai seemed relaxed and was just looking at his cigarette and the surrounding. As members of Command 1, they were told to sleep in Under Asmara. Mahmud, the soldier who was doing the counting that evening knew who they were and denied their request to sleep outside in the open air. Yonatan kept on begging to sleep outside citing health reasons but was rejected. They slept in Under Asmara that evening but the next morning, an order came from the higher office instructing the soldier to let both of them sleep outside in the open-air. It was done for their protection for life in the under's could prove bad for very well-known eve-droppers.

The next morning, Senai was called for questioning at the office and Yonatan waited near the gate, looking at the office from a distance anxiously. At that very hour, medic Tesfai came in and Yonatan run towards him. He began talking with a stressed tone: "I am not healthy. Everyone has isolated me". Medic Tesfai turned to him and said "Did you do good thing to them to expect a good thing from them?" and ignored him.

Upon arrival, Yonatan had found shelter with a former Sembel prison buddy named Shiden (who was on cover of People and Police magazine for stealing 1million Nakfa). Shiden was part of the water distribution crew and squeezed Yonatan in the water distribution role. Senai was suffering from diarrhea most of the time but in the times he was not sick, he was going to work with us. I admit; Senai was smart. Despite his reputation, he had made many friends and stayed active.

Generally, the questioning was more towards Yonatan. They were sure it was only him who did it but they wanted to hear his admission. At some point, both of them were called for questioning by lead investigator Tesfaldet. Tesfaldet turned Yonatan's right arm to the back and turned it around as though he was squeezing water out of a washed cloth. Yonatan, the guy who was doing the beating until then, had found his fate. He had screamed as laud as all the prisoners he tortured over the years and his arm was broken. He was forced to use bandage and rags to keep his arm in place and reduce the pain. After so much interrogation, he admitted to Senai's innocence who returned back to Asmara. Yonatan had said to another prisoner: 'I am sure they have given me at least three years'. May be it is out of good conscience or the realization of the hard truth that he will stay in the prisoner with the very people he tortured, he began asking for apology through Priest Adam to every prisoner he had tortured in his powerful times. Ironically, Priest Adam was badly tortured by Yonatan, too but was forgiven.

Senai didn't get back to his job with Idirs. Instead, he became a typical soldier in division 59. Those people who know him and Division 59 were very well aware of his desire to return to his post but for some reason, he was rejected the opportunity.

Members of Opposition Forces in Ethiopia

They were known and treated just like any other prisoners but there were members of the opposition forces stationed in Ethiopia. Only I and one another person knew about them. They entered Eritrea for their own mission but were caught on suspicion of been smugglers; an accusation they denied but were jailed anyway. They really have fooled the so called unbreakable web of Eritrea's security and existed just like any other prisoner for long. While I don't personally believe they were gathering anything important during their stay in Hashferay, I can't stay for sure what they were doing daily. They had strange memory of dates, however and I often depended on them for dates. One time, one other member was caught and brought to Hashferay. He told the veteran prisoner, who told me in confidence: "We thought you were caught and killed". I can't say whether these prisoners are out or not nor give any other detail for their security but I do thank them for believing me enough to share the dangerous truth.

RELIGION AND FAITH IN HASHFERAY

It is a public secret how many Eritreans had seen their life ending in prison due to their personal faith. Hashferay wasn't the only military-related prison to detain prisoners of faith. The government had uncovered every rock to make something personal a social thing; believe in faiths that they dim are right and accepted. As such, one of the missions of Command 1 in Asmara was locating and detaining followers of those so called "illegal faiths". Those caught were directed almost immediately in Hashferay. The prison was diverse as far as religion was concerned. There were born-again Christians and Jehovah's witnesses from the banned faiths. Everyone went on practicing his own faith with absolute freedom. Bible study sessions were common in under's. Gospel songs, from Orthodox and Born-again Christians, were sung every evening. There was absolute respect and silence when one faith is praying in groups too. In general, the tolerance and acceptance of other faiths was very much respected. The lack of freedom that has brought many to Hashferay in the first was almost non-existent in Hashferay.

However, that wasn't the intention of Hashferay Prison or Command 1. They were kept blind of the activities because no-one reported a thing to them. There was an incidence in early 2013, when one idiot prisoner reported Christian activities of some born again Christians, who were placed in shoe then transferred to Aderser prison. The tolerance was rooted in understanding it is a personal matter and knowing what waits to those followers of the banned faiths. After all, we had a common enemy and no amount of religious difference could fill that gap and hatred we had.

Until June, 2013, Orthodox Christians and Muslims were praying loudly after 7pm in the under's. The guards outside could clearly hear those prayers but didn't order us to stop. One evening in June, the soldiers' realized the number of prisoners that night was fewer from the number of the previous night by one. They were faced with a prisoner that escaped but didn't know who he was at all. They began going from under to under, ordering house leaders to count all prisoners. They would compare each under's number with the previous and decide. The order came at 7pm, when in some under's Muslims were praying Salat prayer while in some Orthodox followers were praying.

Our door was knocked hard but the soldier outside and Wedi-Ele, our house-leader couldn't agree because of the loud prayer. "Tell them to halt the prayer temporarily", an order came to Wedi-Ele who wasn't brave enough to pass the order to the praying Muslims. Wedi-Ele kept on telling the guard the number is the same but they weren't satisfied. Thus they ordered him to count us all, which he accepted but decided to do once the prayer ends.

They came back one more time to find us uncounted and they became mad with anger. Keshi realized the numbers didn't match up and came to their aid, because he was really feared. He first came to Under Titanic and started screaming: "Where the hell do you think you are! This is not a church, this is prison. You stop it right away and we will deal

145

tomorrow. I will see if your God will free you!"

Wedi-Ele ordered the Muslims in prayers to stop their prayer. Next morning Keshi called all the house leaders and ordered them to never have the prayers any more. Even though the rather loud evening prayers were stopped, group bible studies continued. Ironically, followers of the banned faiths had more fear of been reported outside Hashferay. Still we sung gospel songs at the top of our voices every night.

There were few bibles that rotated around in the prison. At some point, pages of a bible were carefully and categorically cut off and rotated among those who needed it. Many had come to know about God there. I have seen cigarette addicts getting free after joining a bible study program. All in all, the factor of religion continued to be part of our daily life.

I myself have learned more about God and Christianity there from bibles and teachings I borrowed from Christians. Many of my Christian poems were written in Hashferay.

Prisoners of faith were treated and punished just like the rest of us. The only difference was that their freedom was in their hand. Followers of the banned faiths can go to the office and swear that they have abandoned their faith and get their freedom. No one had done that at all. Once there was a prisoner named Michael, from Keren. He was a Pentecostal follower. Michael had mental issues that required him to take pills to remain sane and calm. He was in there for two years and as time went by; his mental issue began taking control of him and led to some degree of insanity. He began talking out loud and walking to the exit gate. He was been looked after by prisoners Abrihiley and Solomon. As it was getting worse, they asked Keshi to report the case to the Office. After Keshi reported the case, Abrhiley and Solomon were given the green light to somehow contact Michael's parents so that they can come and take him home.

Michael's father came to Hashferay with his brother and one Orthodox priest. In the office, the mentally absent Michael took an oath on the Orthodox bible denouncing his faith and returning back to Orthodox faith. Michael did leave Hashferay but he had no idea how he did it or what happened. Even though no sane follower had done it, it is essentially the way they get their freedom. That makes their jail period indefinite.

Many times, they transferred religious prisoners to Aderser prison where they work in the bakery, finance and other jobs. That was done with the full knowledge they have no intention of escaping and are generally expected to be faithful in their assigned posts. There was little chance of denouncing their faith, meaning they are likely to hold those positions for long time.

Let me mention a few of the faith prisoners I recall.

Father Adam

Father Adam was educated in Alexandria Orthodox Church, Egypt and followed Orthodox in its strictest form. He was caught by agents of Idirs in Asmara and was put in Villiago's Command 1 torture villa known by "da Idirs". He was tortured there severely. The guard who tortured him the most with whips and rods was Yonatan, who became a prisoner himself later on. During the beating, Father Adam was constantly reminding him "I did it for you, for your future" but Yonatan and the others were full arrogance and stupidity that blinded them from seen the truth and what they were doing.

I didn't confirm it from him directly but someone close to Father Adam told me he was put in jail for he questioned the authority of the Orthodox Pope, who is illegitimate in the eyes of the Orthodox tradition and community.

He came to Hashferay in his usual pope, black gown, with a hat and a cross in his hands. He looked at the place and the first thing he said was: "This is excellent. It feels like a monastery. I will preach the gospel here". And he used to teach some followers after lunch sitting in one of the trees. Keshi began to notice his activities and his clothing and felt uncomfortable.

One Sunday in January 2014, right after the midday count, Keshi ordered everyone to remain seated. "Either you give this priest some clothing or I will give him military clothing!" Some prisoners immediately brought him trousers, shirt and t-shirt. Right then Keshi ordered the priest to take of his priestly gown and take the clothes. Then he turned to Fish, another member and instructed him to bring the Cross from Father Adam. Fish approached Father Adam, as ordered but stopped a few steps away. "Take it yourself Keshi!" Keshi immediately went to Father Adam and took the cross away. That time, Father Adam said "this is just wood. You are not taking my God or faith".

Some elders later went to Keshi and asked him it is not good to take the Cross and he should give it back. Keshi ignored their plea and they returned back empty handed. That Sunday evening, Keshi suddenly felt ill and had to be rushed to the medic. He had severe vomiting and he was shivering a lot. It continued for three days but a controlled rate. I am not qualified to pass judgment over what caused his sickness but he did return the cross right away after he had fallen sick.

There were other prisoners of faith who had dedicated their youth to the country but that didn't matter at all.

There were two Catholic Fratellos' or brothers' from the Catholic Church of Keren (Brother Tsehaye and his colleague) caught when trying to escape to Sudan. They were deeply loved and respected in Hashferay for their extreme and unbiased kindness towards the needy. The imprisonment of them had shown the power of the Catholic Church or the deep connection of Anseba Region with Command 1. They were released within two months. The administrator of Zoba Anseba, Mr. Gergis, a Catholic himself, came on his land cruiser and took them with him from the gates of Hashferay. Their release was well accepted for they were truly kind prisoners. But it reminded us of the deep discrimination running the country.

On March 29, 2014, minibus arrived from Asmara with 10 prisoners. Among them were prisoners Semere and Daniel, who were sent to their families for a few months thanks to the power of their fathers. They returned back now to complete the rest of their sentence. They weren't the highlight of that trip though. The last prisoner to step out of the minibus was a mother, in her sixties, dressed up in traditional Zuriyia dress and had no bag at all. Later that day we confirmed the mother was prisoner of faith.

When I remember the issue of God in Hashferay, what comes to my mind immediately is Gospel song by Yonatan and Sosuna titled "Carried me until now". The song was popular in all the Under's for it represented the reality as it was.

SLAVERY IN HASHFERAY

Hashferay wasn't the first prison to start engaging prisoners on daily works. In fact, it is an expected action. The core difference is that it is mandatory in Hashferay. In other prisons, it is optional and very much a privilege for it means leaving the compound into the open air and gain some sort of experience. Moreover, prisoners who work constantly earn some privileges such as good sleeping spots, shoes, bath after work etc.

Hashferay had no such privileges at all yet the place of work is harsh, demanding and goes on throughout the week during the hot day hours. Until April 2013, prisoners were working from 6:30am until 9am only. Even then, only prisoners who have been through the army were forced to work. The work was mostly gathering stones and had no real meaning. The first major task was building the biggest under there – Under Nakfa.

From April 2013, everyone was forced to work and the working hours extended from 6am until 4:30pm with a mid-day break for lunch and mid-day count.

Building Hagaz Earth dam

The earth dam project of Hagaz was a turning point in our lives. It still remains the biggest project Hashferay ever did and one that brought so much change, misery and hardship to prisoners.

The earth dam requested a huge amount of manpower for no machinery was involved. It was a project supported financially by the Anseba region while Hashferay prison would supply the necessary manpower and project management. As such, prisoners were classified into two groups: one group work two shifts (6:30-10:00AM and from 2:00PM until 4:30PM) and one group composed of mainly the oldest ones from 10:00AM to lunch time.

Hagaz administration participated in the project by providing its own 10 masons and a project manager. On the first two days, a dozer was sent to unearth the area where the foundation could be stationed. From that onwards, there were no sign of machine at all. It required an enormous amount of big stones from the nearby mountains. The project was badly managed from day one and took away all the little energy we had ever saved somehow.

The project was given high priority and attention by Hashferay because all previous earth dam projects in Anseba Zone had failed. A successful earth dam project would become a source of pride for Command 1 and Hashferay in particular. Secondly, it could be an example that Hashferay has an internal capacity to carry out big projects. And of course, there is the popular profit each high ranking official makes mostly in terms of stealing building materials funded by the administrations of Anseba Zone or Hagaz Administration.

Today, it is a 12 stairs high and hard to imagine it was entirely built by human power without the use of any machinery in the 21st Century. It is located on the river the goes from Anseba to Gash Barka region.

Before the building started, Hashferay had to prepare for the task properly. The earth dam was 1km away from our compound and escape attempts could happen. So, before the project started, new army units were brought and stationed around the earth dam for constant look up. The second concern was the possible contact of prisoners with the civilian masons of Hashferay as well as the highly probable interaction of prisoners and guards. They knew they had to create something.

The devil can produce only devil ideas, right? They came up with evil idea. They gathered up the masons and the new guards. "Prisoners will participate in the project. But they are not typical prisoners. They are human traffickers. They have sold Eritreans' like goods. So, any kind of interaction is not allowed". It was the perfect excuse to implant hatred because at that time human trafficking had become a daily occurrence in Eritrea and traffickers were badly hated.

It worked very well. The masons isolated us. The guards took their anger on traffickers on us. Even while carrying a massive stone on our bare shoulders, we weren't allowed to slow walk. Punishments came in their meanest and harshest forms by the guards who thought they are punishing criminals. The punishments included rolling down the hills which were full of stones and thorns; rolling on the burning sand and of course the endless kicks and floggings.

Very fortunately it was short-lived. The masons were the first to learn the truth after they met Prisoners from the town of Hagaz who were caught when escaping the country. That led to curiosity then enquiry and finally, to the truth that it was a bunch of lies. The guards soon realized we were just trying to escape the life they were forced to live every day and their hatred was soon changed to brotherly love. They kept their role to guarding from a close distance without so much other care. That all eventually led to cooperation. The earth dam had physically killed us but it also opened the opening for us to be in touch with our family. The masons were highly cooperative and helpful and would take messages from us and deliver them faithfully. In time, they began bringing us items and messages. They knew they weren't allowed to be messengers but in the words of one of the Masons: 'They can do anything they want. You are our sons'. I can't thank the courage and love of this masons who risked it all to keep us connected to our loved ones.

The earth dam was entirely built with stones and cement. Since it didn't have steel, its chance of standing firm depended on the size of the stones and cement it was taking. And that was our misery. The near-by Mountains were full of stones but unearthing them, carrying them down-words on our bare backs and shoulders and putting them in place was very hard. The distance easily reached 1km, especially as the nearby stones were unearthed. On my first day to join the task, I was barefoot and on strict order to bring big stone. My difficulty started climbing up one of the mountains and finding a big stone I can lift on my shoulders. The stones were hot and putting them on the shoulder as well as holding it in place through both hands brought the idea of hell to my mind. But my troubles were waiting for me when I came down to the plain area down the mountain where guard Goitom Wedi Keshi was waiting and inspecting.

It took me my all in all to bring the stone down and it passed the inspection. When we were told to finally carry our stone to the earth dam, someone left an even bigger stone and disappeared with a possibly smaller stone. Been new, I was delayed in leaving. Wedi Keshi saw my stone was smaller than the stone left behind and he ordered me to take it instead. I looked at the stone and knew it will simply crush me to the ground. "I can't carry this one", I told Wedi-Keshi. Been one of the most mean and rude guards, he simply told me to point my back to him and he whipped my ass as hard as he could. "Carry it!"

"But that's not the stone I brought." I pleaded as soft as I could. "I don't care!" he kicked me once again. "It is too heavy for me. I can't carry it", I pleaded again and got three whips but he let me carry the already heavy stone I had carried down the hill.

Such scenario was common. It was an everyday occurrence for a fairly big stone to be labeled as small and one has to return all the way up to bring a new, bigger one. We had to go up and down for a dozen times in our bare feet and with constant pressure and order to hurry up.

The earth dam requested 100-140quintals of cement each day. As it came to be known, it was the cement earth dam. Hundreds of prisoners had to be lined up to mix and transfer that cement. So, three groups of 12 mixers where lined on the back side while one group on the front side. Each mixing group had members to transfer the mixed cement. To do that, those transferring agents had to be in pairs, going from the ground until the stair been built. Cement would be placed on a sack and be thrown from pair to pair until it reaches the top then the sack would be thrown down to the ground for circulation again. Those prisoners who transfer cement from the mixers to the masons were mostly new as no one wanted to be there at all. The problem is that the frequent friction between the sand and the bare hand often causes wounds and bleeding to the hand. It was also a tiresome job for one group had to transfer 20-25quintals of water-mixed-cements to a stair as high as one's height. I was assigned to the position at least five times and the first part of my body that pained was my stomach for we had to bend down to lift a sack of cement dropped by the pair below us and throw it to the stair above us. Often, we had to beg our way out and be replaced by someone having a crack-free hand. The only good advantage of it was that the guards were in distance and hence one don't have to be worried of a whip, a feet or a flog falling on his back. A common view of those cement transferring prisoners was the lack of shoes. Cement mixed with sand was all over for them to step on. It was a good thing the cement had water; otherwise the heat would have busted open their feet, which was cracked and thin-lined due to exposure to the cement. One of those days, I recall a young prisoner said to me: 'You can't walk bare-feet on this floor. Here, just stand there and hand me over whatever I ask you'. He was right hand man of the major masons and I became his assistant with no job other than to pretend to be active on duty. He was transferred to another prison shortly after but he did make my day that day because truly, my thumbs were bleeding and my feet had started to hurt.

There were two groups that deal with sand. One group would go to the river and load incoming trucks with sand at least four times a day. The other group was around the earth dam, passing sand to the mixers as they need it.

The majority of prisoners were with stone. Their number was so high than the rest that they ended up been known as "China's People". As they move around carrying stones in often a long line, they appear to be a colony of ants. The sides of the earth dam were smoothed by using specially crafted and amazingly big stones. A group was assigned to those stones under the name "da Pele". They were privileged group that worked efficiently with no interaction from the guards and were generally free of pressure.

The most disturbing of the job was however the presence of Keshi in the workplace. He was unbelievably annoying, loud, demanding and can't tolerate the view of any prisoner taking a second to take a deep breath. He was unique in that he barely touches a thing, always clean, always neat but had the capacity to disturb the entire workforce at the pick of his face. His assistant Beleza was no different but often he would grab the spade, help the masons or carry one hell of a stone on his shoulders. And more than all, he would be satisfied at some point, unlike who had issues of admitting the goodness in a task.

The building of the earth dam would remind any side viewer slavery in all its sense. We had masters we had to obey at all times, no questions asked. We had to sweat and bleed for all their sake. We had to labor by hand in the sand with our every move controlled and watched. Of course, we differed in that we knew sooner or later, we would be free.

There were no safety majors at all but miraculously, there was almost no accident. The project was leading itself, not by the human mind. It was why it was very much clumsy and really took longer than it needed.

In May 29, 2013, the long suspend transfer of members of Defense Forces from Hashferay to Adi Abieto prison restarted. 59 prisoners were transferred. Most of them were working in the privileged but hard positions of cement mixing, big stone unearthing and stone breaking. I joined a group that was unearthing big stones and it was the best position I ever had there. It was done on a treeless spot so soldiers would often be away, sitting under a tree while we joke and work at our own pace. It was a bit from the earth dam, thus freeing us from the nagging of Keshi. It felt really different to see 'China People' transferring the stones we just unearthed under tight control and battering by the guards.

We had several visitors during the building of the earth dam; Tekle Manjus, Dehab Fatiniga (the Singer), Ms. Halima (from Hagaz Administration) and administrators of Anseba Region. My most memory was what Ms. Halima said when she saw the hurtful and tough work conditions we were exposed: 'Oh my sons! Oh my sons!' Those were the words she was repeating for the brief minutes she was there. That day, she had come with a Cameraman, probably from their Media department to film the project. He started shooting right away but then Beleza interfered and told him not to shoot or to shoot only the civilian masons.

Generally, the earth dam is remembered in the mind of prisoners by the amount of energy and time it required. It was not a small project by all means yet no machinery was involved at all. It was why we used to say to the prisoners who came after the earth dam was completed: 'You are lucky you weren't there when we built that earth dam' or for the soldiers to say 'You are calling this a job! You obviously haven't seen how the earth dam was built'. I have no doubt each prisoner would tell his own personalized history or memory from it. Let me share with you some of the unique things I still recall.

Once two prisoners were with 'China People' and transferring those hot stones in the afternoon. They were tired and the hot stone had started to remove skin from their necks and shoulders. To have protection, they took out their shirts and put it on their neck. At some point, they noticed the guard wasn't around and so decided to sit down and take a breath. Suddenly, the huge and often mindless Beleza appeared from the middle of nowhere. He burned with anger and started shouting: 'We are working our asses off and you are taking rest! Take out your shirt and lay on your back on the sand'. After 10am, the sand is very hot and the sun from the above is no less. One of the prisoners put his hand on his eyes but Beleza removed it with his legs. He probably had things to do but he stood there with them for thirty minutes, to make sure they don't cover their eyes or worse move around somehow. They appeared to me as fish frying over a grill. He left them there until the day was called off at 4.

One day, cement was over suddenly. Cement is at the center of the job so no cement, no work. Keshi can't tolerate a day where prisoners are free from work. That was often out of the question. Then he looked and gathered 24 of us and assigned five soldiers to accompany us to the storage unit located 2km from the earth dam. Each one was to bring 50kg of cement on his shoulders. Amra, member of Division 63, stood up for a very young prisoner: 'Keshi, he is a kid. He can't carry a 50kg for this long'. Keshi for once listened to a complaint and returned the kid. Amra also talked to him on my behalf but Keshi replied: 'I don't care, I don't care. All of them would refuse to go! Just get me the cements immediately now'. He was right; none of us wanted to walk for 2km in the burning sun. The soldiers were sorry for us. The one on the right side: 'Are these people or animals?' Of course, they had no power to do anything except obey orders, just like us. Very luckily, as we reached the storage area, a water tank was going to the earth dam from there and we loaded it up with 50quintals against the will of the driver thanks to Beleza's authorities. Beleza was quite heartless when it comes to prisoners. He enjoyed the view of struggling prisoners (carrying something heavy) and would laugh so laud. But that day, an angel must have fallen on him.

My most and last memory was the importance of cement sacks. It was valued more than the prisoners. After each cement is opened for use, its suck is carefully counted and kept. We struggle to steal them because we could wash it and make it part of a sleeping bag. The loss of one sack could trigger a thorough search among us. Many were successfully stolen and ended up becoming wonderful sleeping bags. It makes me smile to remember and type it now; the struggle we had to go through to steal a cement's sack and how one smiles after he sneaks it in.

The earth dam of Hagaz was inaugurated on June 26, 2013. That morning, 20 prisoners were selected from Under Tessenai. They were all muscular and were given brand new garage overalls. They were taken to the earth dam alone at 8 in the morning. Soldiers of Command 1 were also given the same kind of clothing. They were mixed up and created a work force that looked no close to prisoners. That was a stunt for video shoot out. They returned the prisoners at 9am before official visitors came to the earth dam while the soldiers continued taking the credit for building the earth dam. The video was shown on the national television under the headline 'Hagaz earth dam built by members of the Public Army, Students and Youth of Hagaz and the People of Hagaz'. On July 07, 2013, Hadas Eritrea newspaper published the same lie. But as one prisoner joked: 'Tekle Ewir (blind) has made the entire nation a public army. By extension, we are his army'.

The people of Hagaz knew the truth of course. They sent us memorably delicious food that included meat, rice and Injera. We deserved it but more than all, we were really in need of some quality food.

That wasn't the end of the earth dam however. The earth dam wasn't perfectly lined on the top hence water was falling to the left side, instead of the center. We restarted working on it again in 2014. That time, Keshi wasn't part of the project and it was very peaceful. The job was just increasing the height of the left side by 1meters. It took a week and in that week, the masons from Hagaz had brought in a lot of items, messages and money for us. On the very last day, Saleh Zebra saw some masons giving prisoners stuff and reported the case to Beleza, who ordered the checkup of all of us. "This is our last day. I will let you have everything except anything pepper-based".

The sad thing about the rebuild was that many names written by former prisoners on the top level were removed and destroyed. A few written on the right side remained untouched and safe like "B2" written by my friend Bereket to mean "Bereket Berhane".

In August 2013, the rainy season arrived and the earth dam proved its importance to Hashferay prison and the nearby villages. From that moment on, we started washing our bodies and clothes every week there. It was obviously unsanitary for used water was returning to the river and we would reuse it to wash our bodies or clothes again. But miraculously, no one was sick in relation to the water that was getting contaminated day after day.

The collected water had brought a new, never changing job with it as well. That job was fetching water to water the plants found in the compound, near the offices and pretty much all around. It was a daunting task and one we hated most because we had to do it every day, including holidays and Independence Day. One person would carry 20liters of jerry can back and forth at least 4 times for a distance of 1.5-2km.

Frankly, despite the fact it had brought unbearable misery, hardship and punishment to us, it felt a great sense victory to see water falling from it in that rainy season. Though we built it but no one acknowledged our role, it was nice knowing it will be useful for the future and someday, somehow, someone will tell the truth of who really built that earth dam.

Building the Water Storage Unit

Clean water was supplied to prisoners and the whole Hashferay community via water distribution truck. The truck was old and often required maintenance. When that happens, we were forced to fetch water from a well built within the Hagaz River. It was far and distributing it to all locations was often brutal. The administration wanted to solve that problem by building a water storage unit on top of a hill found behind the compound of the prisoners. Then, tubes would be installed that run down from the storage unit as required.

The storage unit was decided to be built entirely with black stone. Since it was an inside project, the masons were all prisoners. The unit wasn't small; it was meant to store 250,000liters of water.

The gathering of stones started early. The mountains near it were cleared of stones; thanks to the earth dam we just finished building. Hence, we had to look on the completely opposite side, as far as 3-4km. Once again, only big stones were demanded. It was decided that all of us who been through the army would go first, climb up the mountain and carry the massive stones down the hills and mountains then carry them as far as 700m. Another group would carry them for another distance and then civilians would carry it some distance and the last group would carry it up the hill to the spot of the storage unit. Ours was the longest in distance and the hardest but it helped that we had to carry the stones downwards at least. Sure, one had to be very careful when walking for any bumpy step could trigger a fall and crush of the person carrying it. There were many accidents in which a prisoner would suffer a broken bone due to such accidents. But it was harder to carry it up the hill because the hill was made up smooth soil, requiring extra effort to stay stable and strong.

In almost two months, we gathered stones that could form a new hill. Once cement and steel arrived, the masons had to prepare. As the masons were prisoners, we expected some sort of sympathy or understanding but they really didn't. The first thing they said was 'They have gathered useless stones'. So a new mission of removing the stones from the hill started. We had to carry every stone we carried up the hill to the other side of the hill and downwards, which was exhausting and disappoint. We had to gather stones that are 'naturally fit able'. I had no idea about building but later, new mason prisoners from construction companies of Command 1 showed us no stone is useless. Those meant the prisoners building the dam were too lazy to craft or make an extra effort to find a room for a given stone. Hence, we had to gather an entire set of stones for additional two weeks.

The project lacked total management and so, its building extended for longer than necessary. Sunday was picked as the day to lay down the foundation. It took at least 500 prisoners and all the guards close to 10 hours to finish the job, all thanks to bad management and the inability to lead the project.

There was enough stones and cement and man power. There was no logical explanation as to why it took this long. Everyone was exhausted. The platoon caller of that day was Tafla, who after lunch was too exhausted to do anything except sit down in the shade himself. Many prisoners were part of groups that were fetching water from the dam and carry it up the hill for use in mixing the cement and sand. They were hurt the most because not only the distance was long but finding replacement man power became tough for them. Ironically, Tafla ordered many prisoners to lay down in the sun as they didn't come out to work as ordered when the water fetchers were too tired (to the point some crushed to the ground) and in desperate need of replacement.

All man power was oriented to the storage unit until it was finished. Its closing cup was also a major task and done on Sunday. That time, prisoners took charge of the project lead by prisoner engineer Ghrimay and it was smooth, requiring less man power and was done by 10:45AM.

The building of the water storage unit didn't exhaust us as much as the earth dam did. It had a direct use to us because once water was stored; the first beneficiaries were us, the prisoners. We wouldn't have to fetch water from the wells anymore; instead we would just carry it downwards in jerry cans for a much less distance and with much less effort.

After it was built, the question how to fill it up was naturally raised. The water truck had to find a way to climb up the short but steep hill somehow. Once again, the commanders of Hashferay decided that we, the prisoners, will pave a road that goes from the hill to the left side, encircling the prisoners' compound and join a path behind the house of division 63. It was about 1-2km in a straight line.

It wasn't a pretty good job to imagine but fortunately, the mechanical unit of the Defense Force Anseba Region provided a dozer that paved a way on the right side of the dam, a short but steep road. It saved us a lot of trouble. That day, we were standing along the path, removing any stones found on the way or unearthed. Dimo was standing close to us with a project manager who came with the truck. We heard him say: 'We gathered and crafted all this stones by ourselves'. The project manager looked disgusted and replied: 'Stop it! It is not a good thing to say'. I wasn't surprised the headless Dimo said so with so much pride but was surprised and happy at the response he got.

In the end, the old water truck was too weak to drive up the hill and we started filling the storage unit by jerry cans now and then. I didn't stay long to actually see it been full but I have no doubt future prisoners had dealt with the daunting task of filling it.

Building New Prisoner House

For reasons unknown to us, the administrators of Hashferay ordered the building of new halls for prisoners. These two halls, however, were above the ground. It has a fairly big compound, fenced by big stones we gathered again. Except for the gathering of those stones, it wasn't particularly hard project.

It was hard for we never knew what it was until December 2013. Rumors were it will be hosting underage and over age prisoners. Another one was it will be used to connect us with visitors face to face. There were many rumors of this kind, which were purely a result of our hopes.

In the end, it created a segregation of prisoners. Those prisoners with crimes dimmed easy or small were transferred to it while the others remained in the underground halls. It was quite heart breaking because those left behind realized they won't be freed anytime soon. Anyone of them who remains with few months of his sentence was getting transferred to the new house as well.

With the exception of sleeping in above the ground houses, there was no real benefit at all. Pretty much all work was transferred to us. However, given their pending sentence and the living situation they were going through, it was a good thing the other prisoners were spared of the hard work. The administration of Hashferay didn't leave them alone from work projects out of understanding or respect but for a total isolation and separation from us.

When we were separated, they were specifically and clearly told they weren't allowed to interact with us. But it was hard to do so since we had to go to their compound to work or meet somewhere. And the guards also remained helpful in connecting us.

Building Brick Production Unit

It is a project that reminded me that deep within their blank head is a small spot that actually does think. The idea to produce bricks was brilliant. The only financial expense was for cement. Everything else was free. Around 80 prisoners were selected to building the brick production unit near the earth dam (so water could easily be reached). It was as big as a basketball field and led by a former disabled fighter known by Wedi-Amine. I have worked under different prisoners in Hashferay and Wedi-Amine was the worst of all. He had the most bitter tongue and bad temper. I hate to say it but he had the habit of handing over his fellow prisoners to Keshi and the others to beat and punish. The work was for the most part boring. May be it is because we compare projects with the building of the earth dam, the project seemed too easy and too little.

I don't much to say about it but every time I remember it, I remember a prisoner named Eyobel. It was March 19, 2014, 4pm. We finished work but there were some unused bags of cements. We had to carry them back to our halls and a group of 3 prisoners were assigned for each 50kg of cement. It wasn't heavy and we have gotten used to the distance by then.

Eyobel was new and like many of us from Asmara, he was never exposed to labor intensive works. It was his turn to carry the bag and the minute it laid on his neck, he crumpled to the ground. He was embarrassed but his group was supportive. But Keshi and the other guards following insulted him a lot and made fun of him. For the first time, I saw a grown man cry like a little boy. He didn't stop choking and tearing even when we entered our halls.

That incident triggered the mental issues he had always suffered and he became out of control. He would never sleep, day and night; talking at the top of his lung, cursing, begging, laughing and all other things a mentally disturbed does. He had to be chained with iron in his hand for he was becoming physically violent.

He was caught for planning to escape the country by the infamous criminal Idirs. The administration had enough of him and called his mother finally to come fetch him up. On March 31, his mother came to take her son, who was completely out of his mind in a scary appearance to his home. We saw her put new clothes on him and touching his face and giving him all the motherly love she can show. The always talking and shouting Eyobel was quite at the hands of his mother. It wasn't hard to imagine what the dear mother went through at the view of her son that moment.

INNOCENT PRISONERS

I personally don't consider any of the crimes reported in Hashferay as crimes with the exception of those few linked to human trafficking. But it is foolish to expect legal way and understanding from a government which don't understand the meaning of the law and operate in a total lawless style. Every Eritrean has lived and existed under the umbrella of this lawless regime. Many have been treated as goods and placed in jails with a simple yet powerful order: 'Keep him here until I collect him'. Command-1 led by the lawless Tekle Manjus took it a step further and created a chain of unlawful puppies which terrorized the nation and imprisoned anyone they wanted or suspected.

Command 1 was able to control the whole nation using eve-droppers and snitches it implanted within each sector of the society. It collected as much intelligence as it could about our every move and word. Rumor has it that for every information they report, those parasites were rewarded certain amount. May be it could be considered a legit activity to jail someone for finding him planning or attempting to escape. But what can be said of those once who were jailed after the snitches implanted an idea (of escape or other) into your head then accuses the person of accepting it? The prisons of Hashferay were full of such unfortunate prisoners.

What used to surprise me and others was the paralysis of Eritrean Police. It is if they have officially handed over their role to Command 1. People with civilian cases, such as fighting in bars, were been kept in a military prison with no clear accusation or sentencing.

Let me share with you four prisoners who were as innocent as a child. There were many others with similar stories but hey, the government of Eritrea is called lawless for a reason.

Tareke (Hagaz)

Tareke, from the nearby town of Hagaz, was in his early 20s. He left to Nakfa training camp after a year of imprisonment. Here is why. A boy named Dali was going to Asmara to bring some youths to be smuggled to Sudan. On the way to the bus station, he accidentally met Tareke. He said 'I want to go to Asmara but am short of 100nfa. Can you lend me?' Tareke, knowing it is just a typical friendly thing, gave him 100nfa without a word. Sadly, Dali was caught and during interrogation he mentioned the 100nfa. They tracked down Tareke and jailed him reasoning 'you lent 100nfa to a smuggler. You had a role in it'. Tareke had no idea about Dali's intentions but in a court where he had no say at all, he had no option but to be jailed for a whole year.

Amit (Police)

Amit (his nickname) is a 3rd round veteran soldier who participated in all the 1998-2000 wars, continuing his national service with Eritrean Police. At the time I was leaving Hashferay, he was finishing his second year of imprisonment and going to the third year.

He was stationed in Barentu at the time of his capture. The incident is as follows. One day he met an old friend in Barentu. It was around 5pm and they had dinner together. His friend told him that he had a wedding in one of the villages after Barentu and that his bus is already on the way. And they were separated with no out of the ordinary chit-chat.

True, his friend had a bus but it was somewhere in Barentu waiting for dusk to fall down. It was loaded with young people escaping to Sudan. As planned, they started heading out of Barentu but before they went too far, his bus had a problem. Knowing the danger it posed, the smugglers had to act fast. The maintenance needed spare part and he called Amit to bring him the needed spare part quickly. Amit, been friendly and all innocent, bought the spare part and went to the bus. He returned back quickly without checking the bus at all.

The bus was fixed but caught by Command 1 security agents half way. The smugglers mentioned the car's problem and how it was fixed. When they were asked how they got the spare part, they mentioned Amit. Amit was caught and accused of supporting smugglers. He resisted the accusation, stating 'he told me his car was broken and needed a spare part. What was I supposed to do?'

And for that, he was in jail for two full years. There is a chance he might have been freed after May 2014.

Mr. Yigzaw

A father in his sixties, Mr. Yigzaw was a farmer in the nearby villages of Hagaz. He was very social and outgoing man who enjoyed joking around. In Hashferay, he continued working in their farm.

In 2012, there was a successful escape by smugglers. One of the escaped ones wondered in the darkness and ended up in the farm of Mr. Yigzaw. Mr. Yigzaw wasn't in his farm the night the prisoner arrived. But his employees were there. The prisoner looked like a guest and they gave him shelter for the night. Mr. Yigzaw came the next day and just like any father would do, he welcomed the prisoner as his employee and even bought him shoes. He let him stay for three days and said his good byes. Of course, none of them had heard about the break out of Hashferay that time and that he was a prisoner.

It is this love he showed, out of complete innocence, that put Mr. Yigzaw in prison for 2 years (I don't know if he is freed or not).

The escape was so hot and shocked Command 1. So, they tightened up security checkpoints to the highest. The escaped prisoner was a fool in that he boarded a bus and headed towards Barentu. He was stopped at security check point and was tortured. During the torture, he revealed Mr. Yigzaw gave him shelter for three days and gave him shoes. Mr. Yigzaw was accused of cooperating with an escaped prisoner and put to jail.

Khalid (Sudanese)

Khalid, 12 year old, is fully Sudanese. His mother came all the way from Khartoum on March 31, 2014 with his birth and nationality documents and took him out. He was jailed for about 4-5 months. He only spoke Arabic and was in complete stress throughout his time. He had only one gown clothing and at some point, he suffered from skin condition. Some prisoners took the step to gathering money and clothing for him. His crime?

There were many Eritreans in the Sudanese town he was living in from the town of Keren. He heard them say "Keren Tseada" ("White Keren") a lot and with time, he started to be curious why it is called White. That curiosity developed into a childish decision to board on a bus and come to Keren and sees what the fuss was all about. He was stopped in security checkpoint of Tessenai. He was charged on suspicion of been a smuggler or linked to one.

TRICKS OF COMMAND 1 AGENTS

Agents of Command 1 differed from agents of the National Security in almost all levels. The most crucial difference was that National Security agents kept their identity a secret. One day, Idirs, the main agent of Command 1 in Asmara went into Bar Mask with a pistol in his right and a handcuff in his left hand as a sign of dominance and power. They weren't professionals in their job, all which originates from the fact that they didn't take any training, had no idea about their role and how cheap they looked in the public's eye.

Everyone knew the tricks those agents use to catch people and put them in prison. But we kept on doing the same mistakes over and over again and fall to their trap. The most common trick lies in their ability to hide their identity and completely to gain our trust. Of course, that's what any undercover agent does. While sometimes it is hard to suspect who is an agent and who is not, there are general signs. Who would guess the famous singer Dehab Fatiniga was a puppy of Tekle Manjus and had her fair share of jailing and freeing prisoners? Who would guess many girls of Division 59 (located in Central Zone) are eve-droppers for Command 1 yet they look as innocent as the next girl? Even when we are told, we let our personal judgment rule over the fact and get in trouble.

One afternoon, I was reading 'Youth' magazine published by National Youth and Students Union when Senai came and stand by my side. There was an actress advertising condoms in one of the pages and he pointed out to her 'Would you have guessed she is with us and was in one mission to capture some guy with me?' I took a hard look at her; she did successfully conceal her other job. But still I wasn't sure. Senai briefed me about that mission: 'She played the role of a gold buyer when we wanted to capture the guy who was selling gold in the black market'.

And that technique was their main weapon in capturing anyone who wanted to escape the country in search of freedom and better life. I use to hear about Dehab Fatinga was affiliated with the criminals of the country but always had difficulty believing it. My excuse was 'they just wanted to insult her name because she is famous'. I learned of the truth about her at least when we were in Under Tessenai and the guards said she is 'his' (Tekle Manjus). And later, one of their own agents admitted 'She and her son work with us. If she wants to free you right now, she can with just a phone call'.

So, basically, many of us were falling into their hands because we let our personal judgment control us and we stop been objective. We just ignore what we hear and don't have any suspicion over the agents. Sometimes, they leave no room for us to suspect a thing.

Let me share with you a few cases that captured my interest.

Case of Amharay and Eve-droppers Senai and Michael China

Senai, around 30 years old, is a turn-boy from the town of Ela Bereed.

He was a turn boy for busses that go to Barentu and beyond mostly. As stationed in Keren, he became a cheap agent for Abdu, the main security agent of Keren that time. I have heard how the turn boys and how snitches use the bus stations to spy on new faces to the city of Keren so I was not surprised about his status. In fact, once two teachers were captured in Hagaz. They knew they were in trouble when they gotten off the bus in Keren and a young girl started following them. Once they stepped into a minibus to Hagaz, they saw her pick up her mobile and a call, looking at the Minibus. Sure enough, their minibus was pulled over and they were pulled over. It might be hard to imagine that this turn boy's work for the agents but the reality is they do.

Michael China is from Keren. He is typically quite, which is not the behavior of Command 1 puppies but he was nevertheless active for Abdu. These two agents ended up in Hashferay prison. The story is the following:

There was a smuggler nicknamed Amharay. He is from the tribe Bilen and quite tough. His younger brother was kidnapped by human traffickers in the Sinai dessert when going to Israel from Sudan. The traffickers were Eritreans and called Amharay, demanding one million Nakfa. 'I don't have that amount of money' Amharay replied. The talk eventually led to Amharay telling the trafficker in charge he smuggles people from Eritrea. 'Good. You take my brother from Asmara to Khartoum and I will send your brother free to Israel', the trafficker created a deal accepted by Amharay. Amharay had no time. He quickly gathered young men to be smuggled and prepared the traffickers brother. That time, the vehicle he used to smuggle people were in maintenance.

Amharay confided to Senai, who he knew for a long time, all that was going on and how he needs a vehicle to at least smuggle the traffickers' brother. Senai asked for 40,000nfa for his cooperation in bringing a car and Amharay agreed.

Senai quickly turned his back and told Michael china what happened. It was a big case to hand over a smuggler to Abdu. But they decided to play even Abdu by splitting the 40,000 and not telling Abdu about it.

The day of escaping arrived finally. All the escapees gathered in Keren and by dusk, they hid in one area while Senai and Amharay waited for their car to come. Senai had assured Amharay someone is bringing the car. Sure enough, Michael China appeared from the side of the street with a vehicle. Amharay was startled at the view of Michael: 'That guy works for Abdu'. 'No, no...don't worry. He is with us on this. Don't worry' Senai assured Amharay. The escapees were told to be loaded onto the car and Amharay gave Senai 40,000.00nfa and drove off their site. But a few minutes later down the road, Abdu and his men stopped the vehicle and Amharay was captured with his group of escapees. Amharay knew immediately he was been setup.

During interrogation, he told Abdu the whole truth. Abdu told Amharay to call the trafficker in the Sinai then took the phone from him. "This is Abdu, from National Security of Keren. We have got your brother so immediately release those you have captured". The trafficker was much relaxed and replied 'Really? You have handed my brother to the government, no problem. He will be released soon but you will never see your brother again'.

Amharay's brother lost his life in the Sinai desert and Amharay was put in the shoe of Hashferay. After a few days, he asked for interrogators of Hashferay for a chance to talk and he was granted. He told them how he had given 40,000.00 to Senai. And that brought Senai and Michael china to Hashferay.

Amharay, as a smuggler, was in shoe until he was transferred to Aderser prison. When it was time to go to pee in morning and afternoon, he would search the compound in search of Senai and grim his teeth. Senai, who was sleeping in Under Titanic, was living a scared life. He very well knew the minute he got out, his life is in huge danger.

Amharay and his family have no idea about the person who actually murdered their son in the Sinai desert but they do know at least the two people who led the way to his killing.

Yonatan and the Gold Case

In the late 2012 and early 2013, Asmara had become a hub for the trade of gold dug illegally in the mountains of Eritrea or imported from Dubai. Command 1 had confirmed the case and set a plan to capture as many gold traders as possible. So, they gathered all their agents and gave them the order of capturing the gold traders.

One of the agents was Yonatan, who was imprisoned in Hashferay with his colleague Senai. Yonatan immediately remembered a man named Ali. He met Ali in Sembel Prison when he was jailed for theft and Ali for illegal gold trading. He knew Ali was released from Sembel prison and contacted him. By then, Ali had abandoned the gold trading business and was leading a normal life.

When they met, Yonatan said 'My sister is planning on becoming a trader to Dubai. Please get her gold to sell in Dubai.' Ali was startled and told Yonatan he had left the gold business and has no desire to step feet in prison again. But Yonatan continued begging him firmly and finally convinced him. Ali said he will get him gold.

As promised, Ali brought enough gold for Yonatan on their second meeting. Yonatan showed up with one of Idris's puppies playing as his sister and got hold of all the gold Ali brought. Just a few minutes later, Idirs and his men came and arrested Ali on the case of gold trading.

It comes as no surprise that Yonatan decided to trick and jail a former prison-buddy. For him, it is all about the reputation and appreciation by his masters, no matter what. He staged the entire drama and did get what he wanted. Ali was completely fooled. Of course, it is hard to expect Yonatan had become a liar for the most criminal Command of the country. It was harder to believe he would force someone, someone he been through a tough prison life with him, into a wrong doing and put him in jail.

Poet Fessahaye

Fessahaye (Fish) was a wonderful and talented poet who came to Hashferay in January 2014 from Asmara. He was a presenter of poems on Sunday program of Eri-TV. He was fed up with the life in Eritrea and decided to flee the country. He and his friends from his neighborhood started planning their exit. What they didn't know was one of the girls in the plan was Idris's puppy. They have known her for a long time and she was one of their close friends. She was one of the key players in the plan, following up their meetings and offering her ideas.

They settled on a date to leave Asmara and got together. When the time arrived, Idirs and his men came with their car and gun and captured them. She was the only who wasn't captured, marking her relationship with the gang. Fish was very careful not to mention her name but he used to repeat how he learned from his mistake and not to trust any more.

Mission accomplished. That's what the dictatorial regime had worked for since day one; to plant mistrust between the people.

Fish was sleeping with us in Hall Mendefera (one of the newly built halls) and entertained us with songs, jokes and poems every night until he was taken to Nakfa training center.

The Immigration Scandal

It is one of the most awesome groups I had ever met. They were all from Asmara and I very much loved them since the day I met them. The cell existed from around 2009 to December 2012. It was carefully formed and included employees working in the Exit Visa department of

Immigration, the Passport Unit and the Exit control in Asmara International Airport. Due to the complexity of the situation and the number of people involved, I didn't really get the exact story of what happened. But Senai did tell me how they got the ones involved in the making of the passport alone.

While it is not known how the first person to be captured was unknown, at least the capture of Bereket Weldegebriel (China) was known. Senai had a central role in his capture. Senai had a close friend from childhood named Dinar. One evening, they were talking just as normal friends and Senai mentioned how he was fed up with the life in Eritrea as a soldier of division 59. Dinar, been unaware of Senai's job, told him that there is a way to get a passport and leave the country legally.

It was big information for Senai. And a mission was setup to go to the heart of it and get hold of the passport. Senai was assigned for the mission and in the next meetings with Dinar; Dinar told him it will cost him 25,000.00nfa.

Dinar told his master Idirs he needs 50,000 and he was given. Eventually Senai got his passport. He has met the person in charge of making it, Bereket, who was working in the passport division.

Senai had completed his mission of obtaining the passport. And he led Idirs to the arrest of Dinar and Bereket. Following that, many others were arrested in connection with the case.

It wasn't a complete surprise that Senai betrayed his childhood and longtime friend Dinar into torture and prison for long time. But even more stupid was how he said he had given Dinar 50,000. Dinar was bitten and tortured by Idirs and his men to return the 50,000. Dinar said Senai gave him only 25,000.00. Senai was there, watching, as Dinar was been tortured.

At some point, he spoke. 'Leave him. I took the other 25,000' Idirs ordered him to say sorry to Dinar for the torture his lies caused but it was too late.

I hope someday someone will tell the whole story of the Immigration case. For sure, I feel I was told enough but it doesn't seem complete. It was a cell that shook the immigration department. The news has reached the dictator himself directly. It was such a big win for Command 1 in arresting employees of the National Security directly.

When many prisoners were been released from Hashferay to their respective army units and ministries, all those who were caught in relation to immigration remained there, including my dear friend Bereket.

As you saw in the above four cases, the tricks they used were pure lies and manipulation. They target people they know very much and have strong relationship with because they know they are already trusted. The worst remained however them inputting words into your mouth and jail you.

ESCAPE ATTEMPTS

Hashferay is not really easy to escape from due to its location. The presence of armed people in all the nearby villages complicates the matter further because they are trained to respond when warning shots have been fired from Hashferay. The distant location of the prison from densely populated areas fastens the capture of escaped prisoners. Any prisoner who been through the famous prisons of Mai Edga or Adi Abeto would tell you how helpful it is to be jailed near a big town because once one runs, he can disappear into the houses. Every Eritrean knows the painful life of prisoners and so, sure they give shelter with open arms.

True, hundreds of prisoners could break out at once, especially from the work place. But such things need cooperation and trust between prisoners. Though we were all under the same tortures power, there is no doubt there were prisoners who would report such escape plans.

That doesn't mean prisoners never escaped from Hashferay. But it is few compared to the huge number of prisoners there. There were real occasions when escape is at its easiest pick. It was more than common for two armed soldiers to accompany 20 prisoners as far as Hagaz. It is very logical for these prisoners to overpower the guards and run. It was never done. While I can't give concrete reason why it never happened, I can imagine it is because some of us believe our sentences are short and we will leave freely. It is a common knowledge that unity is the key factor in such ideas or plans and I highly doubt we had that. Let me share with you the handful of escape attempts in Hashferay.

Successful Escape of December 2012

It is one of the most beautifully executed escape attempts in Hashferay. Twelve prisoners in shoe cell number 4 made the major escape that shocked Command 1. After the escape, guards were deployed on the north section of the compound too.

The shoe cells were close to the northern fence. The fence is relatively short and there were no guards on that front. I don't personally believe they discovered the truth about the absence of guards in that section at night on their own because they are exposed to sun light for less than 20 minutes during day light only. They must have been tipped by someone, a prisoner or a guard. Once they knew it, they began making a hole in the roof of their cell. The roof is made up of soil and trees; unearthing it couldn't be that hard but it is not something that can happen overnight. The roof is almost level with the ground that any crack or sign of opening is visible to the guards.

They finally made the whole and crawled out. They were all smugglers with at least three years waiting for them. The guard came the next morning to take them out for their morning pee and the cell was empty. Later on, only one was captured as the rest disappeared never to be seen again.

Successful Escape of Bilenay on June 2013

It is not as glamorous as the escape of December 2012 but it was an excellent one. We were working in the earth dam of Hagaz. I was in one of the groups passing mixed cement from bottom to top. Bilenay was in the next group, to my left. He was one of the most hardworking people I have met there. We finished work at 10am and we had to be counted for return. It was noticed one prisoner was missing and it seemed too late fire warning shots or look for him.

I still don't know at what time he disappeared or if anyone had seen him disappear. Given the dozen of guards watching our every move from every corner, it is baffling how he found a way out. Nothing is confirmed but chances are he got help from one of the guards who let him pass easily somehow.

Failed Escape Attempt of Mr. Omer Ali

One of the oldest and weakest prisoners, Mr. Ali was jailed because he assisted two of his grandkids escape to Sudan by letting them stay in his house and show them the way. He was seriously sick man who often had trouble controlling his poop. Mr. Omer Ali is a BinAmir Tigre and spoke Tigre only.

On May 24, 2013, Mr. Ali decided to escape. We were free from work on that day because it was Independence Day. The soldiers were relatively relaxed, expecting a party of some kind at night. At 10:00AM, we were called to pee and he went out just like anyone else. But after he peed, he didn't return back and stayed where he was. The guards found out they have lost one prisoner when they counted the returned prisoners and fired two warning shots to the guards on the top of the mountains and in all directions of the prison.

Mr. Ali forgot to consider that the prison don't stop its daily routine of watching after prisoners. He was caught and returned back. We expected them to beat him but that time; the guards looked at him and didn't act on him. But they returned him to sleep in Under Titanic from the open-air.

The 80 year old Mr. Ali was sent home on March 09, 2014.

Escape of an Eastern Command Soldier

He is one of the prisoners that came on July, 2013. He was member of the Defense Forces, Eastern Command, in garage overalls. The short soldier was odd and barely talks with people, including soldiers of Eastern Command he knew from before. He was sleeping in under Titanic. One Sunday morning, exactly after four days he arrived, he disappeared when he left to pee with a hundred other prisoners. He was in clothing colored as the soil of Hashferay so it was easy for him to look like the ground. His tiny body must have aided him in finding a small hiding place in an otherwise plain area. In any way, his escape was not successful but caused conflict between the soldier who counted the prisoners when they left to pee and the soldier who accompanied them to pee and had to count them back on return. They couldn't agree on the exact number of prisoners they exchanged. Aboy Efrem was in charge that Sunday and from the look of his face, he was convinced his men, the soldiers, had something to do with the escape. In fact, during one of the many counts done that day, he was heard saying to Wedi Ele, house leader of Under Titanic 'I really want to know how he was able to escape'. There was no way to ever find out how he escaped but that odd soldier did fool them in efficient way.

Failed Attempt by Shoe Prisoners (28/08/2013)

August 1 – August 30, Hashferay enjoyed good rain fall. August 28 was an exception. There was no rain that day. Rainy days are perfect cover up for escaping hence we were relatively relaxed from the endless slavery jobs for the whole month.

That afternoon, we were preparing to get our dinner and wondering around the compound. Shoe prisoners from shoe number 6 and Agordat were outside to pee. They were been guarded and accompanied by Hasebela, one of the youngest guards in Hashferay. Inside, Wedi-Fichel was screaming at us to get in line to get our dinner and get water. Tesfai was on the main outside security post, watching our every move.

I was near the water tank, getting water when suddenly guns started firing. I looked towards Tesfai and saw him firing towards the sky. Wedi-Fichel turned to us and started shepherding everyone to get into any under. He was soon accompanied by few other soldiers I didn't have time to look at. But I still don't forget how Mokie left the compound in complete silence and went to sit down on the bed near their sleeping hats. He obviously didn't want to put his hand in what is obviously going to be a bloody incident.

I run to my then under Under Nakfa. We began talking with each other and the only question that we asked each other was 'Do you think they will succeed?' The compound outside our underground was completely quite but soon we heard noise of truck. We climbed up the tiny holes in the bricks of our halls and saw some of the escaped prisoners returning back. After nearly 30 minutes, they let us out and one by one we began to see more of the escaped returning.

Many of prisoners were saying they didn't choose the right time. For prisoners like them, who see the day light only 20 minutes a day, there is no right time. It is very obvious they wouldn't be allowed outside their shoes during rain. They gave it all they could but lady luck wasn't on their side. Probably the only short coming of their attempt was not getting information to which direction to run. Because many were caught heading towards the road. I think they forgot to consider the presence of armed public soldiers in every house hold in every single village of the country.

As we get lined up to eat our dinner, we saw all but two were returned. That time, the officer was Bilenay, who had no history of torture. But that afternoon, he was doing the beating alongside Wedi-Fichel and Hasebela. The beating was hard to imagine. Hasebela himself was putting his feet on the head of the prisoners and smash it against the ground. Many of the prisoners were screaming at the top of their voices as they crawl on the ground non-stop with every beating on their backs and asses.

During the beating, one thing happened that none of us expected. Just like Mokenin, the stone-headed Ismael walked away from the sight and left the compound without hitting a single prisoner.

Many of the prisoners started cracking up and soon, two prisoners were completely isolated and became the target of Bilenay's questions and the beating of Wedi-Fichel and Hasebela.

The two prisoners were Wedi-Keshi and Kubrom. Wedi-Keshi was a smuggler to Ethiopia, while Kubrom to Sudan. They were targeted because the other prisoners said they planned the escape and that Wedi-Keshi at some point said 'I will take gun from the guards'. Of course, the latter part is something that came to us from the soldiers themselves and it might be false. But we knew they were held responsible for the plan and suffered the most torture. To this day, I haven't seen a person who endures punishment and torture with absolute resistance and silence as Wedi-Keshi. He never moved nor talked. It was as if each of the beating that falls on him was just a pat on the shoulder. Though we didn't hear the exact words, Kubrom was talking a lot.

I recall prisoners from Tessenai cursing at Kubrom for cracking up and talking a lot. 'We don't do that. We endure!' Of course, that could be arrogance talking alone. Just because Wedi-Keshi absorbed it completely doesn't mean everyone can. The worst part is that Kubrom's talk didn't help him at all. In the end, he got the same treatment as Wedi-Keshi.

Both Wedi-Keshi and Kubrom were isolated in one shoe and handcuffed with iron bars. The beating continued early the next morning, with all eyes and hands targeting Wedi-Keshi and Kubrom only. Once again, Wedi-Keshi was as strong as an iron bar. They weren't allowed to get out even to pee for the first two days. All the six holes that let air into the shoes were blocked with blocks of plastics. And for the next three weeks, they were fed nothing but a cup of tea and bread.

One evening in the first week of September, the door of the shoe Wedi-Keshi and Kubrom were held was been knocked hard and repeatedly. The guards on watch ignored it completely. When morning came, Ismael opened the shoe to find Kubrom dead. It was Wedi-Keshi who was knocking all night as his cellmate was dying slowly. Kubrom was wrapped up in a white sheet and taken out of the compound to an unknown burial ground. Wedi-Keshi remained isolated for nearly two months. He was physically deteriorating but his spirit and determination was still solid rock.

The escape attempt wasn't entirely a failure. Two prisoners did manage to escape, never to be caught. One of them had a long record with Hashferay and rumor has it he was in for at least a decade.

The escape attempt introduced a new rule to Hashferay. Shoe prisoners were forced to pee in newly built toilets within the fenced compound.

INTERROGATORS OF COMMAND 1

As with any military prison of Eritrea, interrogators of Command 1 were not professionals and practiced the use of excessive force as the only way to cross-examine prisoners. They all have blood in their hands, which has disabled their ability to travel and move around freely. Their movement is often careful, not because they have secret to hide or are important officials but they don't know from which direction the hand that will kill them will come from. These corrupted officials had danced above the law and beyond in torturing and killing many Eritreans'.

Tesfaldet

Tesfaldet, my interrogator, is the lead interrogator and head of all the rest interrogators of Command 1. His main office was in Hashferay but he had office in Under Tessenai as well. Fully hairless, muscular Tesfaldet is usually seen wearing black eye glasses and sandals. He moves from place to place in a sanctioned white pickup Toyota. Tesfaldet talks in low and soft voice which makes it hard to imagine he has broken many bones and destroyed many lives. Unlike the other interrogators, Tesfaldet don't jump into physical violence right away. But when he does, he is the most mean and heartless of all. But his worst characteristic is the mean role he plays in the sentencing of prisoners.

Interrogators play major role in the sentencing of prisoners. There is a committee that follows a set of rules to sentence prisoners. That committee depends highly upon the portion of the interrogation report, specially the section called "Interrogators Opinion". Tesfaldet is known to write the worst opinions about prisoners, giving them an extended sentence.

Tesfaldet is said to have started his interrogation profession by our cook Mussie. Mussie was shot in his leg during his capture and Tesfaldet was poking the unhealed wound with sharp objects to get Mussie to talk. Mussie also lost the inability to hear through his left ear thanks to a hard slap he got from Tesfaldet.
He was the main reason Mussie got five years in sentence.

Tesfaldet was very much feared throughout Command 1. Practically, he was on top of Dimo. However, he is much better and kinder than Dimo. He had a firm saying "they have committed crime and they are getting punished. Do them all things prisoners deserve". He was not against sick prisoners from going for higher medication to Glas Military Hospital. He doesn't enjoy torturing prisoners once they are sentenced. His interaction with sentenced prisoners was extremely limited.

John Cena

Named Tedros (some said his name is not Tedros), he got the nick name John Cena after the wrestler John Cena for his violent behavior and technique. He asks one or two questions and jumps into kicking and hitting with his bare hands, feet and any other material at his disposal. He was never tired of hitting prisoners and it can be safely said that no one who been through his questioning time has gone without some sort of beating. I wasn't able to get the most accurate name of his town but multiple prisoners did assure me he is from the town of Adi-Keyih.

John Cena, though extremely violent and hurtful, is credited for been much better in this Interrogator Opinion report. That's why smugglers he interrogated are subjected to the minimum jail sentence set forth by the judging committee.

Okubay

He had a dark history with prisoners in Aderser, where he did most of his work. He was violent but more shocking, suggests the maximum jail sentence for prisoners he tortured to the judging committee. As such, many prisoners who been through him are still in Aderser while those who got captured after them are released now and then because they got the minimum jail sentence.

Okubay was sacked out of his position on charges of corruption. There was a rumor that he also told one doctor jailed in Hashferay his exact sentence, triggering the doctor's escape. Today, Okubay lives in Hashferay but is no more an Interrogator nor have any job. He knows he can't live freely outside the enclosed compounds of Hashferay and so is living a life that is not different from the prisoners.

Wedi – Keren

He is from Ela-Bered but calls himself Wedi-Keren ('from town of Keren'). He is short, dark and a junior interrogator. Following the footsteps of his masters in Under Tessenai, Wedi-Keren uses methods of intimidation right away. He does try to create short, fake stories to try a prisoner to talk, such as saying 'You have been here before; I remember you very well'. He wasn't used to handling big; smuggling cases on his own so often does transfer them to John Cena or Tesfaldet. But just like them, he had broken many bones and hopes

Woldu

Woldu is the only interrogator of Command 1 I have never seen. He was stationed in Asmara and people who know him call him very smart and visionary. He was exceptional in that he applies smart technique of cross-examination and gets what he wants without a single beating. Senai admits that Woldu opposes the way eve-droppers and snitches (like Senai himself) work; he strongly opposed 'feeding people words and ideas then jailing them for saying something or acting on the ideas given to them by Command 1 agents'. Often the orders he gives had meaning but unlike the other interrogators, Woldu wasn't active in the affairs of prisoners, including the ones captured in Asmara.

LEAVING HASHFERAY AND ERITREA

One night in Under Titanic, Wedi Ele said 'we will walk out freely through the door we walked in jailed'. There were many more sayings like 'If Africa is prison, Eritrea is the shoe', 'and Prison is the best university one can ever attend'... they were all true. The longer one stays, the smarter and brave he gets. The life gets boring because it is overly mundane. At one point, my good friend Mike said 'It is really enough now. We are bored'. Well, it wasn't in our hands. We didn't even know our sentence.

Prison is supposed to change the way we think, to regret our actions but the reality was completely different. We had spent endless hours talking about our cases, exchanging experiences, giving tips and making plans to meet outside and do it again in a perfect fashion.

And that's exactly what most of us did. From within the prison itself, we planned our next escape; our next action. On April 1, exactly 11 months later, I was transferred to Adi Abeto prison.

Adi Abeto was my last prison in the series of prisons I stayed in. It was a pretty bad prison itself I do hope someone who was jailed there for long years there tells its story for Adi Abeto had a fair share of its dark history in the lives of Eritrean youth.

I escaped from Eritrea to Ethiopia exactly two months after I left Hashferay. It was a beautiful escape. I have learned my lessons from Hashferay and dared not to do any mistake. Because a second capture would send me for at least 3 years, on top of torture and beating for trying to escape the regime once again.

And there I am now, typing all that I can remember, in the hope of preserving some of Hashferay's history for the future so that those who lost their lives wouldn't be forgotten and those who did the inhumane act wouldn't escape history and hopefully, justice.

ABOUT THE AUTHOR

Sammy Sium is a former prisoner at Hashferay Camp. He was born and raised in Asmara, the capital of Eritrea. He took the mandatory military training in 2002 and have been in the forced national service from 2006 to 2013. He is a computer science graduate and is living in exile after he escaped from his home country in 2014.

Made in the USA
Monee, IL
02 December 2020